Letters of Credit and Documentary Collections

Letters of Credit and Documentary Collections

An Export and Import Guide

Thomas H. Ward, MBA

To order additional copies of this book, contact:
Xlibris Corporation
1-888-795-4274
www.Xlibris.com
Orders@Xlibris.com
55504

CONTENTS

PROLOGUE

This book shows detailed actual examples of the documents that are used in international sales and explains why they are necessary when doing international transactions. After reading this book, you will be able to select the best payment method to protect your business when doing an international sale.

There are several safe methods used to do international transactions when receiving payments for goods or services. They are the following:

a. Letter of credit
b. Documents against payment or D/P
c. Documents against acceptance or D/A
d. Net 30 days based on invoice date or bill of lading date
e. Payment in advance of shipment by international wire transfer of funds

There are different types of letters of credit. A letter of credit does not necessarily mean you will be paid. The type of letter of credit is very important, as are the terms of the agreement. In some countries, like China, you have very little protection using a letter of credit. One United States bank advised me that a Chinese letter of credit is not worth the paper it is written on.

ABOUT THE AUTHOR

Thomas H. Ward, with an MBA in international business, has thirty years' business experience and over twenty years in small business international sales. He started and ran three different companies. He was vice president and director of a major international company. Ward has worked and lived in Asia, with business travel to twelve countries around the world. He spearheaded the first sales into China and Korea in 1980 for three major United States companies. Ward was the first to start export sales, for these companies, from the USA to a number of Korean and Chinese companies. These Korean and Chinese companies had never had any business dealings with United States companies.

INTRODUCTION

I classify international banking and international shipping together because for a international business that buys and resells materials, the two are interrelated. It is necessary to have a bank and a freight agent that has a lot of experience in international business. Do not use a small local bank as they cannot meet your need when it comes to doing business outside the United States. They claim they can, but this bank will just subcontract your business out to one of the big banks such as Citigroup, KeyBank, JP Morgan, and Bank of America. You will end up paying higher fees, and it will take longer to have your paperwork processed and approved. This all means a loss of profit dollars in higher bank fees and communications problems. This can cost you a lot of wasted time. Bank fees can run as high as 7 percent of the transaction value.

The bank you select should have banking relations with the banks in the foreign countries you will do business with, for either exporting or importing. A banking relationship means these banks have established formal business relationships and they know how each other operates. International banks have a list of banks in each country they do business with. For example, if I want to sell to a company in Korea, I must know the name of their bank. Then you need to check with your bank if they have direct relations or indirect relations with this bank. KeyBank in the United States may have relations with Bank of Korea and not the customer's bank, which happens to be Korea Exchange Bank. Or Korea Exchange Bank may have relations with Bank of Korea New York Branch in the USA but not with KeyBank directly. This direct or indirect relationship is important as paperwork and money flow through these banks. If they do not have a direct or indirect relationship, then they cannot transfer documents and funds. Indirect bank relations also cost you more in fees than a direct bank relationship. So it is better if your bank has direct banking relationships with the customer's bank to reduce your banking fees for international transactions.

It is very important to have a shipping agent or freight forwarder that knows how to do international business and has good relations or contacts with the major freight airlines and shipping companies. Your freight agent can make or break your business. Your shipping agent needs to know the international shipping regulations. If he provides bad service and is late with shipments, your company will obtain a bad reputation with the customer. The agent must know how to make a correct bill of lading and then forward this bill of lading to you right away. Your agent must be licensed for air and ocean freight. They also need to be bonded.

The bill of lading is very important as this is the proof that the correct goods were shipped, what date they were shipped, the arrival date, and the name of the carrier. The description of the goods on the bill of lading must match the letter of credit and the invoice description. The bill of lading is a legal document that is necessary to obtain payment from the bank.

There are several safe methods used to do international transactions when receiving or sending payments for goods:

    a.   Letter of credit

    b.   Documents against payment or D/P

    c.   Documents against acceptance or D/A

    d.   Net 30 days based on invoice date or bill of lading date

    e.   Payment in advance of shipment by international wire transfer of funds

CHAPTER 1

Letters of Credit

Letters of credit are one important means of transferring money and paperwork between customer and supplier. The banks act as a trusted in-between. If a seller agrees to be paid by a letter of credit or LC, then you need a reliable bank to handle the transaction. A letter of credit is a type of contract used by banks to protect their customers when doing international business. How do letters of credit work? Letters of credit are established and used when customer and supplier do not know each other very well and there is doubt about the supplier or buyer trusting each other to fulfill the contract. Sometimes an LC is required by the country you are doing business in as a way for the government to monitor trade. Your company or your customer may ask for a letter of credit to be used in any transaction when there is any doubt about either party's ability to pay or supply the goods.

There are different types of letters of credit. The most common types are an irrevocable LC, transferable LC, and irrevocable/confirmed LC. A letter of credit does not necessarily mean you will be paid. To guarantee payment, you need to have your customer provide an irrevocable/confirmed letter of credit. An irrevocable LC is a written credit that cannot be revoked or have any of its terms and conditions changed without the approval of both parties within the time dates shown on the LC. A confirmed LC means the exporter's bank confirms and adds its commitment to honor the letter of credit payment terms to the importer's bank. In this case, as long as all the documents are correct and the goods have been shipped within the time requirements, you will be paid.

A transferable letter of credit is usually irrevocable and should also be a confirmed LC for added protection. A transferable LC is a credit that is assigned as payable in full or partial amount to a third party.

Letters of credit also have ship dates specified, expiry dates, and documents presentation dates. These dates are very important to meet, and if you are outside the dates, the LC may not be valid anymore. It is necessary to have these dates give you as much time as possible to complete the shipment and present the documents to the bank for payment. For example, if the LC has an expiry date of May 26, 2008, and this date passes before you ship the goods, then the LC is no longer valid and the customer and the bank will not accept the shipment or documents for payment unless you can obtain an approval from the customer to change the date to give you more time. The customer would do this through their bank by issuing an amended LC with the new expiry date. If you ship the goods without this, you risk nonpayment. The same holds true for the ship date. If the goods are not on board by this ship date, then you need to obtain approval from the customer to change the ship date or risk nonpayment. One can obtain the customer's approval by having the salesperson contact your customer's purchasing department and advise them that you cannot meet the time set forth in the LC. You need to ask them to amend the LC dates. Usually, the customer will agree to do this amendment. If the customer does not make this amendment, then the agreement is no longer valid.

Typical documents you will need to supply to your advising bank are invoice, packing list, bill of lading, certifications, and bank draft. The bill of lading is the proof that the shipment has been made, and it tells the arrival date. It also describes the goods which need to match the packing list and invoice.

Here is how a letter of credit works. Orion Company and Kemco Company have reached an agreement where Orion will buy from Kemco one million dollars worth of steel rod. Orion in Korea imports steel from Kemco in the USA. Orion has an account with Bank of Korea. Kemco has an account with KeyBank in the USA. In this example, we assume these banks already have an international relationship, which means they can do business with each other.

Kemco, the seller, and Orion, the buyer, agree to LC terms as an irrevocable/ confirmed LC with payment terms on acceptance of documents. Kemco also advised Orion that they need a ninety-day LC expiry date and thirty days for shipment date from the time LC is opened. Kemco is the beneficiary, and Orion is the issuing company. Bank of Korea is the issuing bank, and KeyBank is the advising bank and will advise Kemco and send them the final copy of the LC. The LC is written by Bank of Korea for Orion, and then the Bank of Korea sends it by special carrier to KeyBank, which checks it and sends it to Kemco. Once this LC is sent to KeyBank, that means the money is ready to be paid upon proof of documents and conformance to all the terms of the LC. This is because it is a confirmed LC.

Kemco will use a shipping agent to ship the goods to Korea. The shipping company will issue a bill of lading with the LC number on it and a description of the goods that match the invoice and LC to Kemco. These documents will then to be sent back to KeyBank for their review and approval. Assuming there are no errors or discrepancies, KeyBank will forward the documents to Korea Bank for their approval. If all is OK, then payment is wire transferred to KeyBank, and the documents are released to Orion to obtain the goods from Korean customs. KeyBank puts the money into your business account. This concludes the confirmed LC purchase.

Summary of letter of credit transaction:

1. Your customer agrees to issue you a purchase order, and you both agree on the LC's terms and conditions before the customer contacts their bank. This is very important as you need to put in writing what terms and conditions you require so the letter of credit is written more or less in your favor. This is the time to advise them what you need for the expiry dates and ship date times. This is also the time to tell them what type of letter of credit you require to make the sale and reduce the risk to your company. It is also the time to check if your bank and the customer's bank have direct or indirect banking relationships.

2. The customer will advise his bank to issue an LC with the terms and conditions you have both agreed to. This is the issuing bank. This bank then sends the LC to your bank, which is the advising bank. Your bank will send the original LC to you for review and approval. One needs to carefully review the LC to make sure that it conforms to your original agreement. If the LC meets the agreement, you can proceed with the order. If it does not meet the agreement, you need to e-mail your customer and explain the problem with the LC. You must ask them to change it or amend the LC. If they make the amendment, this change will be submitted back to you by your advising bank. If they do not make the amendment, then you can reject the LC by

returning it to the advising bank, stating in writing why you do not accept the terms and conditions of the LC.

3. If you find the LC acceptable, forward a copy of the LC and your invoice to your shipping agent. Make sure the agent prepares the bill of lading to match the LC's wording and that the freight agent is aware of the necessary shipping dates. The LC number should always be referenced on the invoice, packing list, bill of lading, and any other paperwork. You need to ask your agent by what date he needs the goods or materials at his location to meet the latest shipment date on the LC. The on-board date in the bill of lading must be a date before the LC's latest shipping date.

4. It is a good idea to have two people review the documents before you send them to your bank. Once you have received the original bill of lading, put all your documents together and review them. You are now ready to send them to your bank for review. Make sure you do not go past the LC's expiry date to submit the documents. Your bank will review the documents to make sure they comply with the LC's terms and conditions. If the documents do not comply, your bank will advise you that you have a discrepancy and will ask you to correct it or to go ahead and submit them to the customer's bank (issuing bank). The customer along with their bank can approve or disapprove the discrepancy.

    It is suggested if you have a discrepancy to e-mail the customer for their approval ahead of time. A discrepancy can be just about anything that the banks feel is not in accordance with the LC's terms and conditions. It can be as simple as a misspelled word on the invoice or bill of lading. Banks are very picky on letters of credit wording, and each discrepancy can cost your company about twenty to thirty dollars. This discrepancy fee is in addition to the cost of your bank handling the letter of credit as advised in the advice letter from your bank. Once your bank has approved the documents, they send them by special delivery to the customer's issuing bank for approval. At this point, it is up to the customer to accept the shipment by acceptance of the documents or reject it.

5. Once approved by the customer, their bank payment is remitted to your bank, the advising bank; and the funds are put into your account. The customer can now pick up his goods at the customs broker bonded warehouse. All goods are usually held until they obtain the original documents, which are

released from the bank, showing the goods were paid for by the customer. The transaction is now complete.

You can see why it is important to have a good bank and a good shipping agent. In addition, you need to have a lot of trust in your customer to make good on the payment for the letter of credit. So you must know your customer very well, and just how dependable the company may be is very important.

Letter of credit typical documents that may be required are:

a. The bill of lading issued by the shipping company. This document is official proof that the goods listed in the LC have been shipped or are scheduled to ship. The bill of lading should describe the goods exactly as it appears in the LC. The bill will also show the date the goods are being shipped, the name of the ship or airlines, and the flight number.

b. Your company invoice and packing list are necessary to send with the LC. The invoice dollar amount must match the dollar amount in the LC, and the goods need to be described exactly as in the LC.

c. You will need to make a bank draft, which is supplied by your bank, and it shows the exact amount to be paid on the LC.

d. It is common for the buyer to request a certification or document that proves the goods meet their quality specification.

On the following pages, there is an example of a letter of credit issued by the Bank of China. There is a two-page advice letter from the Bank of China New York Branch. The letter of credit was issued by the Bank of China Jiangsu Branch. For China letters of credit, we found it is best to use the Bank of China New York Branch as the advising bank for LC transactions. This is because the issuing bank is also the Bank of China. And there is direct and fast communication between these banks. So if the issuing bank from a foreign country has a New York branch or a branch in the United States, use the same bank for faster payment. Note that the advising bank does not take any responsibility to assure or promise payment to your company, and neither does the issuing bank on a normal irrevocable LC.

The LC in the following example (page 22) is an irrevocable LC payable by the customer within sixty days after the bill of lading date. These sixty days allow thirty days for the goods to arrive by ship to a China port and permits the customer another thirty days to pay. It is not good to allow sixty-day payment terms. One would rather use payment at sight or payment on submission of documents to the bank in China after they are approved.

It is necessary to read the letters of credit very carefully to make sure it adheres to the terms and conditions you agreed to. Study pages 22 and 23 closely to understand the wording as it is similar in all credits. The important points in an LC are:

a.   The date of latest ship date and expiry date of the letter of credit
b.   Beneficiary, applicant names, and addresses
c.   Drafts, payment amount, and payment date
d.   Type of shipment allowed
e.   Commodity description and price terms and who is paying freight
f.   Type of documents you must submit to the bank for payment

Note the following definitions:

1.   The advising bank, in most cases, is your bank. They advise you or send you the original copy of the letter of credit. The advising bank is just an in-between bank that can help you with problems and show you how to avoid letter of credit discrepancies.

2.   The issuing bank is the customer's bank that has issued the letter of credit according to your customer's instructions. The issuing bank also does not promise payment unless it is a confirmed letter of credit or has a confirmation clause. To obtain a confirmed letter of credit it may cost you up to 3 percent of the proceeds for this protection, but a confirmation is sometimes worth the expense. For the issuing bank to add a confirmation, you must advise your customer that you require a confirmed letter of credit. The customer will not like this as they must put up the full amount of the LC payment in a special account for the issuing bank to hold. Once the documents are received and approved by the issuing bank, they will release the payment to your company right away, less the confirmation charges. This means you can receive payment in less than thirty days if all goes well with the documents.

3.   Applicant: This is who had the letter of credit issued, which is your customer.

4.   Beneficiary: This is you, the supplier. Your company is the beneficiary of the letter of credit payment.

For this LC, there is an expiry date of July 10, 2006. The LC was issued on June 2, 2006 (see paragraph 31C, 31D, and 44C). The latest ship date is June 25, 2006. So you have about twenty-two or twenty-three days to make the latest ship date and about thirty-two days to meet the LC expiry date. Normally one would like to have thirty days for ship date and sixty days for the LC expiry date to be safe. If the LC expires, then it needs to be accepted on deviation or amended. This can cause long delays in payment to you, and if the material has been shipped, you might be waiting a long time to get paid.

On page 23, paragraph 45A of the LC is the description of the goods. This description must be put exactly on your invoice and the bill of lading just how it appears in the LC. Another important point is paragraph 46A, which advises what documents and how many copies of each are required by the issuing bank. If this is not followed, this can also cause a long delay in your payment.

Document examples in chapter 1 are:

Page 20, 21 Letter of credit advice letter

Page 22, 23, 24 Actual letter of credit example

Page 25 Bank draft

Page 26 Application of documentary collection

Page 28, 29, 30 Invoice, packing list, and bill of lading

Other documents required by this letter of credit from China are:

Page 31, 32 Certificate of origin and certificate of quality

Page 33, 34 Declaration of no-wood packing and beneficiary's certificate of packing material

Page 35 Beneficiary's certificate

Page 36 Due date advice letter

Page 37 Advice of payment letter

BANK OF CHINA NEW YORK BRANCH   TELEX: TT7 423635, WU 661 723   S.W.I.F.T.: BKCH US 33

410 MADISON AVENUE
NEW YORK, NY 10017
TEL: (212) 935-3101
FAX: (212) 593-1831

```
BENEFICIARY:                                    DATE: JUN 02 2006
     INC                                        OUR ADVICE NO: AD06NY1421
              BAYWAY SO. 5
              FL
ATTN: MR. RON

ADVISED THROUGH BANK (IF ANY):

LETTER OF CREDIT NUMBER: LC9401250/06

SUBJECT: ADVICE OF LETTER OF CREDIT.          DATE: JUN 02 2006

ISSUED BY: BANK OF CHINA JIANGSU BRANCH

FOR: USD 75,600.00
```

DEAR SIR AND MADAM,

WE HAVE ATTACHED A COPY OR THE ORIGINAL (IF STAMPED ORIGINAL) LETTER
OF CREDIT INSTRUMENT TO THIS ADVICE. SHOULD YOU FIND ANY TERMS AND
CONDITIONS NOT ACCEPTABLE OR INCORRECT, PLEASE COMMUNICATE WITH THE
LETTER OF CREDIT APPLICANT TO ARRANGE THE NECESSARY AMENDMENT. WE
WILL BE HAPPY TO ASSIST YOU IN RELAYING YOUR MESSAGE TO THE LETTER
OF CREDIT APPLICANT THROUGH THE ISSUING BANK.

THIS IS SOLELY AN ADVICE OF LETTER OF CREDIT AND CONVEYS NO ENGAGEMENT
ON THE PART OF BANK OF CHINA, U.S.A

AT TIME OF FIRST DRAWING, YOU MUST RETURN THIS ADVICE LETTER AND
THE ATTACHED LETTER OF CREDIT INSTRUMENT TOGETHER WITH ONE ADDITIONAL
COPY EACH OF FULL SET OF DOCUMENTS FOR OUR FILE. IN ORDER TO EXPEDITE
YOUR PAYMENT, PLEASE ALSO INCLUDE YOUR BANKER'S NAME, ITS ABA NUMBER
AND YOUR ACCOUNT NUMBER ON YOUR COVERING SHEET WHEN PRESENTING DOCUMENTS.

UPON FIRST PRESENTATION OF DOCUMENTS, IF YOU HAVE NOT DONE SO BEFORE,
PLEASE PROVIDE US YOUR TAX I.D. FOR KNOW YOUR CUSTOMER PURPOSE.
PRESENTATION OF DOCUMENT(S) THAT ARE NOT IN COMPLIANCE WITH THE APPLICABLE
ANTI-BOYCOTT, ANTI-TERRORISM, ANTI-MONEY LAUNDERING, AND SANCTIONS
LAWS AND REGULATIONS IS NOT ACCEPTABLE. APPLICABLE LAWS VARY DEPENDING
ON THE TRANSACTION AND MAY INCLUDE UNITED NATIONS, UNITED STATES
AND / OR LOCAL LAWS.

THE FOLLOWING CHARGE(S) (IF ANY) ARE FOR YOUR ACCOUNT :

```
ADVISING COMMISSION                      USD      90.00
```

```
TOTAL CHARGE:                            USD      90.00
```

WE WILL DEDUCT OUR CHARGES TOGETHER WITH OUR HANDLING COMMISSION

BANK OF CHINA NEW YORK BRANCH

TELEX. ITT 423635, WU 661723   S.W.I.F.T.: BKCH US 33

410 MADISON AVENUE
NEW YORK, NY 10017
TEL.: (212) 935-3191
FAX: (212) 593-1831

FROM THE PROCEEDS IF DOCUMENTS ARE HANDLED THROUGH OUR BANK, OTHERWISE
PLEASE REMIT TO US THE ABOVE CHARGES BY WIRE (OUR ABA NO. 0326 UID116246,
FEDWIRE NO. 026003269) OR BY CHECK.
(USD20.00 ADVISING FEE WILL BE REFUNDED AS REBATE IF DOCUMENTS ARE
PRESENTED TO US FOR HANDLING/NEGOTIATION EXCEPT FOR SPECIAL PRICING
CUSTOMER OR ADVISING CHARGES FOR THE ACCOUNT OF APPLICANT)
OUR SCHEDULE OF CHARGES WILL BE SUPPLIED UPON REQUEST.

OUR CONTACT NUMBERS:
FOR LC ADVISING: - EXT. 348 OR 340
FOR PRESENTATION OF DOCUMENTS: - EXT. 346
WE ARE LOOKING FORWARD TO SERVE YOU SOON!

                              TRULY YOURS,

                              BANK OF CHINA NY

(THIS IS COMPUTER-GENERATED LETTER; NO SIGNATURE IS NECESSARY UNLESS
THE ORIGINAL LETTER OF CREDIT IS ATTACHED)

02/06/06-05:26:34   MPFUSMTBOUTLC-0444-028504   1

```
---------------------- Instance Type and Transmission --------------
Copy received from SWIFT
Priority              : Normal
Message Output Reference : 0524 060602BKCHUS33AXXX0053192471
Correspondent Input Reference : 1724 060602BKCHCNBJA9401398751630
---------------------------- Message Header ------------------------
Swift Output   : FIN 700 Issue of a Documentary Credit
Sender         : BKCHCNBJ940
                 BANK OF CHINA
                 (JIANGSU BRANCH)
                 NANJING CN
Receiver       : BKCHUS33XXX
                 BANK OF CHINA
                 NEW YORK,NY US
MUR : JSIMNIM T6464
---------------------------- Message Text --------------------------
27: Sequence of Total
    1/1
40A: Form of Documentary Credit
     IRREVOCABLE
 20: Documentary Credit Number
     LC9401250/06
31C: Date of Issue
     060602
31D: Date and Place of Expiry
     060710U.S.A.
 50: Applicant
     HUA FEI COLOUR DISPLAY SYSTEMS
     CO. LTD., NO.1 HUAFEI ROAD, MAI
     GAO QIAO, NANJING P.R.CHINA
     P.O.BOX 2808
 59: Beneficiary - Name & Address
```

BANK OF CHINA - NEW YORK
REFERENCE NUMBER:
AD06NY 1421

TF 06153-04567

```
32B: Currency Code, Amount
     Currency       : USD (US DOLLAR)
     Amount         :           #75,600.00#
41D: Available With...By... - Name&Addr
     ANY BANK IN U.S.A.
     BY NEGOTIATION
42C: Drafts at...
     60DAYS AFTER B/L DATE
     FOR 100 PCT OF INVOICE VALUE
42D: Drawee - Name & Address
     BANK OF CHINA,
     JIANGSU BRANCH
43P: Partial Shipments
     ALLOWED
43T: Transhipment
     ALLOWED
44A: On Board/Disp/Taking Charge at/f
         ACTORY
44B: For Transportation to...
     NANJING
44C: Latest Date of Shipment
```

060625

45A: Descriptn of Goods &/or Services
COMMODTY: LUDOX AM 36000 KG
PRICE TERM: EX WORKS :   FACTORY

46A: Documents Required
1. SIGNED COMMERCIAL INVOICE IN 3 FOLDS INDICATING LC NO. AND
   CONTRACT NO.125529.

2. 2/3 SET OF CLEAN ON BOARD MULTIMODAL BILLS OF LADING
   PLUS 1 NON-NEGOTIABLE COPY MADE OUT TO ORDER AND BLANK
   ENDORSED,MARKED FREIGHT COLLECT,NOTIFYING THE APPLICANT.

3. PACKING LIST/WEIGHT LIST IN 2 FOLDS INDICATING
   QUANTITY/GROSS AND NET WEIGHTS.

4. CERTIFICATE OF ORIGIN IN 2 FOLDS.

5. CERTIFICATE OF QUALITY IN 2 FOLDS ISSUED BY MANUFACTURER.

6. DECLARATION OF NO-WOOD OR NON-CONIFEROUS WOOD PACKING
   MATERIAL.

7. BENEFICIARY'S CERTIFICATE CERTIFYING THAT ONE SET OF THE
   PACKING MATERIAL MUST MEET THE REQUEST OF CHINA INSPECTION AND
   QUARANTINE AND ONE SET OF NON-NEGOTIABLE DOCUMENTS (INCLUDING
   1/3 ORIGINAL B/L) HAS BEEN DISPATCHED TO APPLICANT DIRECTLY BY
   COURIER/SPEED POST IMMEDIATELY AFTER SHIPMENT.

8. BENEFICIARY'S CERTIFICATE CONFIRMING THEIR ACCEPTANCE OR
   NON-ACCEPTANCE OF THE AMENDMENTS ISSUED UNDER THIS CREDIT
   QUOTING THE RELEVANT AMENDMENT NUMBER,SUCH CERTIFICATE IS NOT
   REQUIRED IF NO AMENDMENT HAS BEEN ISSUED UNDER THIS CREDIT.

47A: Additional Conditions
+ ALL DOCUMENTS ARE TO BE PRESENTED TO US IN ONE LOT BY
  COURIER/SPEED POST. OUR ADDRESS IS BANK OF CHINA, JIANGSU
  BRANCH NO.148 SOUTH ZHONGSHAN ROAD NANJING 210005 JIANGSU
  P.R.CHINA.

+ A DISCREPANCY FEE FOR USD56.00 WILL BE DEDUCTED FROM THE
  PAYMENT FOR EACH SET OF DOCUMENTS CONTAINING DISCREPANCY(IES).

+ AN EXTRA COPY OF INVOICE AND TRANSPORT DOCUMENT MUST BE
  PRESENTED FOR OUR FILE, AND USD10.00 WILL BE DEDUCTED FROM THE
  PROCEEDS IN THE ABSENCE OF SUCH DOCUMENTS.

71B: Charges
ALL BANKING CHARGES OUTSIDE OF
OPENING BANK ARE FOR BENEFICIARY'S
ACCOUNT.

48: Period for Presentation
DOCUMENTS TO BE PRESENTED WITHIN 15
DAYS AFTER THE DATE OF SHIPMENT BUT
WITHIN THE VALIDITY OF THE CREDIT.

49: Confirmation Instructions
WITHOUT

78: Instr to Payg/Accptg/Negotg Bank
+WE HEREBY UNDERTAKE THAT DRAFTS DRAWN UNDER AND IN COMPLIANCE

02/06/06-05:26:34   MPPUSMTBOUTLC-0444-028504   3

WITH THE TERMS AND CONDITIONS OF THIS CREDIT WILL BE PAID AT
MATURITY.
+IF WE GIVE NOTICE STATING ALL DISCREPANCIES IN RESPECT OF WHICH
WE REFUSE THE DOCUMENTS,WE SHALL HOLD THE DOCUMENTS AT YOUR
DISPOSAL.BUT IF WE DO NOT RECEIVE YOUR INSTRUCTIONS FOR
RETURNING THE DOCUMENTS WHEN THE APPLICANT WAIVES THE
DISCREPANCIES,WE SHALL RELEASE THE DOCUMENTS TO THE APPLICANT
ACCORDINGLY.
------------------------- Message Trailer -------------------------
{MAC:E706EA12}
{CHK:25FDDAC5D53B}

Other LC-related Documents

It is necessary to submit an application of documentary collection, see page 26. This application can be obtained by the Bank of China New York. In addition, it is necessary to issue a bank draft, as stated in paragraph 42C and 42D. Bank draft copies for your use can be obtained also from the advising bank.

APPLICATION OF DOCUMENTARY COLLECTION

TO: BANK OF CHINA, NEW YORK BRANCH   DATE: **JUNE 09, 2006**

We enclose the following specified documents. Please collect in accordance with our instructions indicated herein and the rules stipulated in URC 522. We understand that we will be bound by all the rules stipulated in URC 522 and agree to reimburse you for all your unpaid charges and the charges incurred by your correspondent bank in connection with this collection. We also understand that presentation of document (s) that are not in compliance with the applicable anti-boycott, anti-terrorism, anti-money laundering, and sanctions laws and regulations is not acceptable. Applicable laws vary depending on the transaction and may include United Nations, United States and / or local laws.

COLLECTION INSTRUCTIONS ARE MARKED "X":	COLLECTING BANK (in full address):
☐ deliver documents against payment (D/P) ☐ deliver documents against acceptance (D/A) ☐ do not protest ☐ protest for non-payment/non-acceptance	**BANK OF CHINA – JIANGSU BRANCH** **148 ZHONG SHAN NAN ROAD** **NANJING 210005, JIANGSU PROV.** **CHINA** **ATTN: INT'L DEPT.**

TEL.

	DRAWN ON (in full address):
☒ advice non-payment and/or non-acceptance ☒ advice payment ☒ advice acceptance	**HUA FEI COLOUR DISPLAY SYSTEMS CO. LTD.,** **NO.1 HUA FEI ROAD, MAI GAO QIAO** **NANJING, P.R.C.** **P.O.BOX 2808**

☐ collect interest from drawee _____ % p.a. from _____ to approximate date proceeds arrived in _____ (basis of 360 days)	TENOR: at **60** days after B/L or AWB date (due date **AUGUST 13, 2006**)
☐ your correspondent's charges to be paid by drawee	AMT & CURRENCY: **USD75,600.00**
☐ collect your charges from drawee ☐ your charges to be paid by us ☒ waive all charges if refused by drawee and charge them to us *DO NOT SHOW BANKING CHARGES ON COVER LETTER*	DISPOSITION OF PROCEEDS: (X) please remit proceeds by chips through **KEY BANK NATIONAL ASSOCIATION** for credit to our A/C no. **91437** quoting Our reference **5314**

OTHER INSTRUCTIONS:	SPECIAL INSTRUCTIONS:
WIRE PROCEEDS TO: **KEY BANK NATIONAL ASSOCATION** **ACCOUNT NAME: KIA, INC.** **ACCT# 350001091437** **TELEX: 89=5817 ABA# 041001039**	1. Please request the collecting bank to remit the proceeds by telegraphic transfer. 2. All documents will be sent in one cover by courier designated by you unless otherwise stated.

DOCS	draft	Com Inv.	Cust inv.	Pack list	Qty/ Qlty Cert.	Insp. cert.	Cert. orig.	Ins pol/ cert.	B/L or AWB	NN B/L. AWB	Cert. of anal	Non-Wood Cert.	Cust. P.O.
NO ENCL	1	3		2			2		2	3	2	2	1

CONTACT NAME: **MR. RON WARD**   YOURS FAITHFULLY,

APPLICANT: **INC.**
                 PINELLAS BAYWAY SO.
                 SUITE   _____
                        FL   AUTHORIZED SIGNATURE

TELEPHONE NO.:   **727-867-**

THIS APPLICATION OF DOCUMENTARY COLLECTION IS SUBJECT TO URC 522

The required letter of credit documents, items listed in paragraph 46A are listed below and are on the following pages.

These are all the typical documents you may encounter in processing a letter of credit. So you can see, it is very confusing and time consuming. Review the following example documents.

INC

PINELLAS BAYWAY SOUTH,

FL   U.S.A.

TEL:001-717
FAX: 001-717

COMMERCIAL INVOICE

Date	Invoice #
6/9/2006	5314

Bill To	Ship to
HUA FEI COLOUR DISPLAY SYSTEMS CO. LTD., NO.1 HUA FEI ROAD, MAI GAO QIAO, NANJING, P.R.CHINA P.O.BOX 2808	HUA FEI COLOUR DISPLAY SYSTEMS CO. LTD., NO.1 HUA FEI ROAD, MAI GAO QIAO, NANJING, P.R.CHINA P.O.BOX 2808

CONTRACT NO. 125529	Terms		Ship Via	
	60 DAYS AFTER B/L DATE		OCEAN / EX-WORKS	
Description	Unit	Shipped	Price	Amount
LUDOX AM (1322 521 01801) 30 PCS. N.W. = 1200.0KG. EA. / 36000KG. TOTAL G.W. = 1259.5KG. EA. / 37784KG. TOTAL	KGS.	36,000	$210.00	$75,600.00
COUNTRY OF ORIGIN: **U.S.A.**				
Documentary Credit Number LC9401250/06				

ORIGINAL
INC

Total $75,600.00
Payable in
US DOLLARS

COMBINED TRANSPORT BILL OF LADING		Page 1 of 1 v1

SHIPPER	B/L Number: KKLUUS0304386 (COPY)	
INC PINELLAS BAYWAY SOUTH NC FL USA	EXPORT REFERENCES BKG##US0304386 5314	

CONSIGNEE	FORWARDING AGENT - REFERENCES	
TO ORDER		

	POINT AND COUNTRY OF ORIGIN	
NOTIFY PARTY	U.S.A.	
HUA FEI COLOUR DISPLAY SYSTEMS CO. LTD., NO. 1 HUA FEI ROAD, MAI GAO QIAO, NANJING CHINA P.O.BOX 2808	IN ACCEPTING THIS BILL OF LADING, Merchant agrees to be bound by all the stipulations, exceptions, terms and conditions on the face and back hereof, and the terms and conditions contained in Carrier's applicable Tariff, whether written, typed, stamped, or printed, as fully as if signed by Merchant, any local custom or privilege to the contrary notwithstanding, and agrees that all representations, agreements or freight engagements for and in connection with Carriage of Goods are superseded by this Bill of Lading. On presentation of one or more original of this Bill of Lading (duly endorsed) to Carrier by or on behalf of Holder, the rights and liabilities arising in accordance with the terms hereof shall (without prejudice to the terms of this Bill of Lading, or any rule of law or statute rendering them binding on Merchant) become binding in all respects between Carrier and Holder as though the contract evidenced hereby or contained herein had been made between them. FINAL DESTINATION (FOR MERCHANT'S REFERENCE ONLY) SEE CLAUSE 7(1)	

PRE-CARRIAGE	PLACE OF RECEIPT EAST CHICAGO, IN	
VESSEL/VOYAGE 18W CHEROKEE BRIDGE	PORT OF LOADING LONG BEACH, CA	
PORT OF DISCHARGE SHANGHAI CHINA PORT	PLACE OF DELIVERY NANJING, CHINA	

PARTICULARS FURNISHED BY SHIPPER				
CONTAINER & SEAL NO.	NO. OF PKGS	DESCRIPTION OF PACKAGES AND GOODS	GROSS WEIGHT	MEASUREMENT
HUAFEI		"SHIPPER'S LOAD & COUNT" FREIGHT COLLECT PACKED IN 2X40' CONTR. SAID TO CONTAIN 30 PACKAGES COATING SOLUTION/LUDOX AM CONTRACT. NO. 125529 DOCUMENTARY CREDIT NUMBER LC9401250/06 COUNTRY OF ORIGIN : U.S.A.	37784 KGS 83298 LBS	41.62 CBM 1470 CFT

AES XTN : 222645753-5314
AES ITN : X20060605001193

KLFU1348482   2783
KKFU1357599   2784

RECEIVED FOR SHIPMENT 06/09/2006 FREIGHT COLLECT. SHIPPER'S LOAD AND COUNT.
DOOR/CY.

These Commodities, Technologies or Software were Exported from the United States in Accordance with Export Administration Regulations. Diversion Contrary to U.S. Law Prohibited.

DECLARED VALUE $	IF SHIPPER ENTERS A VALUE THE AD VALOREM RATE WILL BE CHARGED (SEE CLAUSE 24)		
FREIGHT AND CHARGES	RATE/PER	PREPAID	COLLECT
O.FRT(14777)	2.000 USD 1,610.00 P40		3,220.00
	PAYABLE AT: NANJING TOTAL:		USD 3,220.00

IN WITNESS WHEREOF, the undersigned, on behalf of Kawasaki Kisen Kaisha, Ltd., Vessel, her owners, operators and charterers, has signed the number of Bill(s) of Lading stated below, all of this tenor and date, one of which being accomplished, the others to stand void. No. of Original Bills of Lading 3	PLACE & DATE OF ISSUE RICHMOND, VA JUNE 09, 2006	KAWASAKI KISEN KAISHA, LTD. ON ITS OWN BEHALF AND ON BEHALF OF THE VESSEL, HER OWNERS, OPERATORS AND CHARTERERS By NON-NEGOTIABLE (COPY) "K" Line America, Inc., as Agents for Carrier Kawasaki Kisen Kaisha, Ltd

INC

PINELLAS BAYWAY SOUTH,

FL   USA

TEL:001-717·
FAX: 001-717·

PACKING LIST/WEIGHT LIST

Date	Invoice #
6/9/2006	5314

Bill To	Ship to
HUA FEI COLOUR DISPLAY SYSTEMS CO. LTD., NO.1 HUA FEI ROAD, MAI GAO QIAO, NANJING, P.R.CHINA P.O.BOX 2808	HUA FEI COLOUR DISPLAY SYSTEMS CO. LTD., NO.1 HUA FEI ROAD, MAI GAO QIAO, NANJING, P.R.CHINA P.O.BOX 2808

	Terms	Ship Via
CONTRACT NO. 125529	60 DAYS AFTER B/L DATE	OCEAN / EX-WORKS

Description	Unit	Shipped
LUDOX AM (1322 521 01801) 30 PCS. N.W. = 1200.0KG. EA. / 36000KG. TOTAL G.W. = 1259.5KG. EA. / 37784KG. TOTAL	KGS.	36,000

COUNTRY OF ORIGIN: **U.S.A.**

Documentary Credit Number
LC9401250/06

ORIGINAL KIA INC.

Certificate of Origin

. Inc. hereby certifies and confirms that all products included in this shipment were made in quality and quantity at factories in the United States of America.

. Invoice # 5314

HUA FEI - CONTRACT # 125529

DOCUMENTARY CREDIT NUMBER LC9401250/06

Commodity	Quantity / Weight
LUDOX AM	30 PCS. / 36,000.00 KG

Original
Inc.

06/09/06

GRACE Davison

W. R. Grace & Co.-Conn.
7500 Grace Drive
Columbia, MD 21044

CERTIFICATE OF QUALITY

Date Printed: **JUNE 9, 2006**
PRODUCT: **LUDOX AM**
DATE SHIPPED: **JUNE 9, 2006**
DATE OF MANUFACTURE: **MAY 30, 2006**

INVOICE: 5314
HUA FEI CONTRACT: #125529
DOCUMENTARY CREDIT NUMBER: LC9401250/06

This CERTIFICATE OF QUALITY, issued by Grace Davison & Co., the manufacture of Ludox AM, certifies that the Lot Number Listed below, shipped to you, meets all specifications.

PROPERTY/UNIT	SPECIFICATION RANGES	LOT NUMBER/ANALYSIS
		2006850371
SPEC. GRAV. @60F	1.199 TO 1.216	1.207
pH@25C	8.6 to 9.3	9.0
%SiO2	29.0 to 31.0	30
%TRANSMISSION	62.0 MINIMUM	85
VISCOSITY@25C	25.0 MAXIMUM	12.2
SURFACE AREA (m2/g)	198 TO 258	227
%Al2O3	0.17 TO 0.21	0.19

Lynn C. Pate
Lab Resource

Declaration of no-wood packing material

To the Service of China Entry & Exit Inspection and Quarantine:

It is declared that this shipment does not contain wood packing materials.

Invoice # 5314

HUA FEI - CONTRACT # 125529

DOCUMENTARY CREDIT NUMBER LC9401250/06

Commodity	Quantity / Weight
LUDOX AM	30 PCS. / 36,000.00 KG

Original Inc.

06/09/06

Beneficiary's certificate for packing material

To the Service of China Entry & Exit Inspection and Quarantine:

It is hereby certified that one set of the packing material used in this shipment meets the request of China Inspection and Quarantine.

Invoice # 5314

HUA FEI - CONTRACT # 125529

DOCUMENTARY CREDIT NUMBER LC9401250/06

Commodity	Quantity / Weight
LUDOX AM	30 PCS. / 36,000.00 KG

Original Inc.

06/09/06

Beneficiary's certificate

It is hereby certified that one set of non-negotiable documents (including 1/3 original original B/L) has been dispatched to the applicant directly by courier/speed post.

Invoice # 5314

HUA FEI - CONTRACT # 125529

DOCUMENTARY CREDIT NUMBER LC9401250/06

Commodity	Quantity / Weight
LUDOX AM	30 PCS. / 36,000.00 KG

Original Inc.

06/09/06

After the documents have been sent by your advising bank to the issuing bank, you should receive a due date advice letter. This advises that the documents have been received and have been accepted. This also advises the date when you will receive payment on the letter of credit. This due date advice letter is issued by the issuing bank, which in this case is the Bank of China Jiangsu Branch.

BANK OF CHINA NEW YORK BRANCH

410 MADISON AVENUE
NEW YORK, NY 10017
TEL: (212) 935-3101
TELEX: ITT 423635, WU 661723   S.W.I.F.T.: BKCH US 33   FAX: (212) 593-1931

```
                    DUE DATE ADVICE
          ---------------------------------

                               OUR FAX NO:  (212) 486-0540
                                            (212) 308-4891

     DATE:  JUL 03 2006

     TO:        INC


     ATTN: MR. RON
           OFFICE PHONE       727-867-
           OFFICE FAX         727-867-

     YOUR REF:  5314              OUR REF:  TF061530456701

     UNDER L/C NO:  LC9401250/06

     ISSUED BY:  BANK OF CHINA JIANGSU BRANCH

     BILL AMOUNT:  USD 75,600.00

     ------------------------------------------------------------

     ATTN : JIM
     FAX  : 717 656
     WE RECEIVED A LETTER/SWIFT FROM THE L/C OPENING
     BANK ADVISING/CONFIRMING THAT THE SUBJECT BILLS
     HAS BEEN ACCEPTED TO MATURE ON: AUG 8, 2006

     IF DOCUMENTS AMOUNT EXCEEDS USD 50,000 AND YOU
     NEED TO DISCOUNT THE SUBJECT BILLS AND RECEIVE
     THE PAYMENT NOW, PLEASE CONTACT MR. KAM YEUNG AT
     EXT. 344 OR MR. NOOR KHAN AT EXT. 346 FOR DETAILS.
     WE HOPE THAT WE CAN SERVE YOU AGAIN.
     THANKS FOR YOUR BUSINESS.


     BEST REGARDS
     ALICE, L/C DEPT
     BANK OF CHINA, NY BR


     IF YOU HAVE ANY FURTHER QUERIES, PLEASE DON'T HESITATE TO CONTACT

     US ON THE ABOVE MENTIONED NUMBERS. THIS IS A COMPUTER-GENERATED LETTER.

     NO SIGNATURE REQUIRED.
```

The due date letter advised the payment date was August 8, 2006. You should receive a payment advice letter dated August 8, which tells you the payment has been made to your account. The below example shows bank charges that have been taken out of your payment for the letter of credit transaction. In this case, the total charges were $346.00. This concludes the letter of credit sale.

BANK OF CHINA NEW YORK BRANCH

TELEX: ITT 423635, WU 661723   S.W.I.F.T. BKCH US 33

410 MADISON AVENUE
NEW YORK, NY 10017
TEL: (212) 935-3101
FAX: (212) 593-1831

```
                    PAYMENT ADVICE
                    - - - - - - - - - - - - - - - - - - - - - - -

BENEFICIARY:                         DATE: AUG 08 2006


ATTN:                                DRAWING NO:TF061530456701

YOUR REFERENCE:  5314

IN SETTLEMENT OF YOUR DOCUMENTS AGAINST LETTER OF CREDIT  LC9401250/06

WE HAVE REMITTED TODAY IN YOUR       *************************
FAVOR ACCORDING TO YOUR              *                       *
INSTRUCTION:                         *  USD75,254.00          *
                                     *                       *
                                     *************************

- - - - - - - - - - - - - - - - - - - - - - - - - - - - - - - - - - - - - - -
* DRAFT:USD 75,600.00   * LESS BANKING      * FOR ACCOUNT OF  *
* NO-LIEN: USD          * CHARGES           * BENEFICIARY     *
- - - - - - - - - - - - - - - - - - - - - - - - - - - - - - - - - - - - - - -
* AMOUNT               *                   *                  *
* USD 75,600.00        *                   *                  *
*                      *                   *                  *
*   @          @       * ADVISING COMMISSION * 70.00          *
*                      * DISCREPANCY FEE     * 50.00          *
*                      * NEGOTIATION COMMISSION * 100.00      *
*                      * COURIER SERVICES    * 50.00          *
*                      * CHIPS/FEDERAL WIRE TRANS* 20.00      *
*                      *                   *                  *
*                      *                   *                  *
*                      * FOREIGN BANK CHARGES * 56.00         *
*                      *                   *                  *
*                      * DISCOUNT INTEREST:  *                *
- - - - - - - - - - - - - - - - - - - - - - - - - - - - - - - - - - - - - - -
* PAYMENT AMOUNT:USD 75,254.00                                *
- - - - - - - - - - - - - - - - - - - - - - - - - - - - - - - - - - - - - - -
* DISCOUNT RATE *          **                                 *
- - - - - - - - - - - - - - - - - - - - - - - - - - - - - - - - - - - - - - -
* FOR    DAYS          *                                      *
* MATURITY DATE:AUG 08 2006  *                                *
- - - - - - - - - - - - - - - - - - - - - - - - - - - - - - - - - - - - - - -
```

BANK OF CHINA NY

(authorized signature)

CHAPTER 2

Letter of Credit Discrepancies

It is normal to always have some type of discrepancy show up after the advising bank reviews your documents. A discrepancy is an error or mistake made on any of the documents that may be submitted. It could be a typing error or a misspelling. The advising bank will review all your documents for any mistakes.

Common Discrepancies

a. The letter of credit has expired.
b. The bill of lading shows the ship date is past the required ship date in the LC.
c. Charges in the invoice do not match the LC amount.
d. Description of the goods does not match the LC.
e. Ports of loading are not as specified in the credit.
f. The quantity or volume in the invoice or bill of lading does not match the LC.
g. Company names in the documents do not match that in the LC.
h. Not all the documents required by the LC are submitted to the bank.

On page 41 is an email letter from the Bank of China New York Branch advising of the discrepancies they have found. In the e-mail, they state the following discrepancies were found and would like to know how we wish to handle the problems. These are discrepancies from the letter of credit in chapter 1. Refer back to the letter of credit in chapter 1, on page 22.

Discrepancy 1 (Refer to page 41)

The invoice and packing list have the wrong fax number shown. The mistake was a type error, and it showed a 565 phone exchange number, and it should have been a 656 phone exchange.

Discrepancy 2

The invoice price terms should say "EX-Works factory," and it says just "Ex-Works."

Discrepancy 3

The bill of lading states the place of receipt as East Chicago, In: but the LC just says it should be "factory." So "factory" should have been used in the space.

Discrepancy 4

Beneficiary's certificate for packing material had one set missing and should have been dispatched by courier to the applicant directly.

Discrepancy 5

The draft had the wrong LC number shown as LC 9401052/06, and it should be LC 9401250/06. The draft needs to be corrected.

When you are advised of any discrepancies, you have two choices: authorize the advising bank to proceed and forward the documents as is to the issuing bank or have the documents returned to you for your correction. If there is enough time, returning the documents to you for correction is the best method. Keep in mind each discrepancy will cost you money. Common fees are anywhere from $20 per item to $100 per item. These above five discrepancies could cost as much as $500.

If the discrepancies are simple ones that do not affect the payment in any manner, then in most cases it is safe to authorize the bank to proceed and submit the documents to the issuing bank. Should you do this, then it is necessary to e-mail your customer with a copy of the discrepancies and ask for their approval to go ahead and proceed with documents submission. This way, your customer will tell their issuing bank to approve or waive the discrepancies so there will be no delay in payment.

The following pages show:

a.   E-mail letter discrepancy notice
b.   Commercial invoice discrepancy
c.   Bill of lading discrepancy
d.   Beneficiary's certificate for packing material discrepancy
e.   Bank draft discrepancy

See if you can find the discrepancies listed in this chapter. In this case, only the draft was corrected, and the other discrepancies were left as they were and sent to the issuing bank and customer for approval.

Document examples in chapter 2:

DISCREPANCIES NOTICE (YR INVOICE NO. 5314 FOR USD75,600.00 OUR REF. ...   Page 1 of 2

Subj: **Fwd: DISCREPANCIES NOTICE (YR INVOICE NO. 5314 FOR USD75,600.00 OUR REF. A...**
Date: 6/26/2006 9:09:27 AM Eastern Standard Time
From:
To:

In a message dated 6/23/2006 4:08:38 PM Eastern Daylight Time, ACHANG@BOCUSA.COM writes:

HI JIM

DOCS PRESENTED WITH THE FLWG DISCREPANCIES

1. INVOICE , PACKING LIST
     - BOTH BENE'S FAX NO SHOWN ' 001-717-565-'
     SHOULD BE ' 001- 717 - 656-

2. INVOICE - PRICE TERMS SHOWN 'EX- WORKS'
    SHOULD BE ' EX-WORKS KIA FACTORY '

3. B/L - PLACE OF RECEIPT ' EAST CHICAGO, IN' NOT AS PER
     L/C '   FACTORY '

4. BENE CERT.
     - PART OF THE CONTENTS OMITTED ' ONE SET OF THE
     PACKING MATERIAL MET THE REQUEST OF CHINA INSPECTION
     AND QUARANTINE AND ONE SET........ DIRECTLY BY COURIER/SPEED
     POST IMMEDIATELY AFTER SHIPMENT '

5. DRAFT - L/C NO. SHOWN ' LC9401052/06 ' SHOULD BE ' LC9401250/06 '

PLS LET US KNOW WHETHER YOU WILL REVISE DOCS OR AUTHORIZE
US TO FORWARD DOCS TO ISSUING BANK ON APPROVAL

PLS NOTE L/C WILL BE EXPIRED ON JUL 10, 2006 AND THE LATEST PRESENTATION
DATE IS ON JUN 26, 2006.

BEST REGARDS

Alice

L/C Dept (Tel no. 212-935 3101 ext 339)
Bank of China, New York Br

INC
PINELLAS BAYWAY SOUTH,

FL   U.S.A.

TEL:001-717
FAX: 001-717

COMMERCIAL INVOICE

Date	Invoice #
6/9/2006	5314

Bill To	Ship to
HUA FEI COLOUR DISPLAY SYSTEMS CO. LTD., NO.1 HUA FEI ROAD, MAI GAO QIAO, NANJING, P.R.CHINA P.O.BOX 2808	HUA FEI COLOUR DISPLAY SYSTEMS CO. LTD., NO.1 HUA FEI ROAD, MAI GAO QIAO, NANJING, P.R.CHINA P.O.BOX 2808

	Terms	Ship Via
CONTRACT NO. 125529	60 DAYS AFTER B/L DATE	OCEAN / EX-WORKS

Description	Unit	Shipped	Price	Amount
LUDOX AM (1322 521 01801) 30 PCS. N.W. = 1200.0KG. EA. / 36000KG. TOTAL. G.W. = 1259.5KG. EA. / 37784KG. TOTAL. COUNTRY OF ORIGIN: U.S.A. Documentary Credit Number LC9401250/06	KGS.	36,000	$210.00	$75,600.00

ORIGINAL
INC

Total	$75,600.00
Payable in US DOLLARS	

COMBINED TRANSPORT BILL OF LADING Page 1 of 1 v1

SHIPPER INC PINELLAS BAYWAY SOUTH NC FL USA	B/L Number: KKLUUS0304386 (COPY) EXPORT REFERENCES KKGR#US0304386 5314
CONSIGNEE TO ORDER	FORWARDING AGENT - REFERENCES
	POINT AND COUNTRY OF ORIGIN U.S.A.
NOTIFY PARTY HUA FEI COLOUR DISPLAY SYSTEMS CO. LTD., NO.1 HUA FEI ROAD, MAI GAO QIAO, NANJING CHINA P.O.BOX 2808	IN ACCEPTING THIS BILL OF LADING, Merchant agrees to be bound by all the stipulations, exceptions, terms and conditions on the face and back hereof, and the same well certificate contained in Carrier's applicable Tariff, whether written, typed, stamped, or printed, as fully as if signed by Merchant, any local actions or privilege to the contrary notwithstanding, and agrees that all representations, agreements or freight engagements for and in connection with Carriage of Goods are represented by this Bill of Lading. On presentation of one or more original(s) of this Bill of Lading, duly endorsed to Carrier by or on behalf of Holder, the rights and liabilities arising in accordance with the terms hereof will (without prejudice to the terms of this Bill of Lading, or any in n all per or whole inclusive) from binding on Merchant) become binding in all respects between Carrier and Holder as though the contract evidenced hereby or contained herein had been made between them. TOTAL DESTINATION (FOR MERCHANT'S REFERENCE ONLY) SEE CLAUSE 7(3)

PRE-CARRIAGE		PLACE OF RECEIPT EAST CHICAGO, IN		
VESSEL/VOYAGE CHEROKEE BRIDGE	18W	PORT OF LOADING LONG BEACH, CA		
PORT OF DISCHARGE SHANGHAI CHINA PORT		PLACE OF DELIVERY NANJING, CHINA		

PARTICULARS FURNISHED BY SHIPPER

CONTAINER & SEAL NO	NO OF PKGS	DESCRIPTION OF PACKAGES AND GOODS	GROSS WEIGHT	MEASUREMENT
HUAFEI		"SHIPPER'S LOAD & COUNT" FREIGHT COLLECT PACKED IN 2X40' CONTR. SAID TO CONTAIN 30 PACKAGES COATING SOLUTION/LUDOX AM CONTRACT. NO. 125529 DOCUMENTARY CREDIT NUMBER LC9401250/06 COUNTRY OF ORIGIN : U.S.A.	37784 KGS 83298 LBS	41.62 CBM 1470 CFT

AES XTN : 222645753-5314
AES ITN : X20060605001193

KLFU1348482   2783
KKFU1357599   2784

RECEIVED FOR SHIPMENT 06/09/2006 FREIGHT COLLECT.   SHIPPER'S LOAD AND COUNT.
DOOR/CY.

These Commodities, Technologies or Software were Exported from the United States in Accordance with Export Administration Regulations. Diversion Contrary to U.S. Law Prohibited.

DECLARED VALUE	IF SHIPPER ENTERS A VALUE THE AD VALOREM RATE WILL BE CHARGED (SEE CLAUSE 26)		PREPAID	COLLECT
FREIGHT AND CHARGES	RATE PER			
O. FRT (14777)	2.000 USD 1,610.00 P40			3,220.00
	PAYABLE AT: NANJING TOTAL:			USD 3,220.00

IN WITNESS WHEREOF, the undersigned, on behalf of Kawasaki Kisen Kaisha, Ltd, Vessel, her owners, operators and charterers, has signed the number of Bill(s) of Lading stated below, all of this terror and date, one of which being one accomplished, the others to stand void. No. of Original Bills of Lading 3	PLACE & DATE OF ISSUE RICHMOND, VA JUNE 08, 2006	KAWASAKI KISEN KAISHA, LTD. ON ITS OWN BEHALF AND ON BEHALF OF THE VESSEL, HER OWNERS, OPERATORS AND CHARTERERS. By **NON-NEGOTIABLE (COPY)** "K" Line America, Inc., as Agents for Carrier Kawasaki Kisen Kaisha, Ltd.

Beneficiary's certificate for packing material

To the Service of China Entry & Exit Inspection and Quarantine:

It is hereby certified that one set of the packing material used in this shipment meets the request of China Inspection and Quarantine.

'nvoice # 5314

HUA FEI - CONTRACT # 125529

DOCUMENTARY CREDIT NUMBER LC9401250/06

<u>**Commodity**</u>   *<u>Quantity / Weight</u>*

LUDOX AM   30 PCS. / 36,000.00 KG

Original Inc.

06/09/06

U.S. $ 75,600.00   JUNE   9   20 06

90 DAYS AFTER B/L DATE – JUNE 9, 2006   of this *FIRST* of Exchange (Second unpaid)

Pay to the Order of   INC.   Bayway So.   Verde, FL   U.S.A.

SEVENTY FIVE THOUSAND SIX HUNDRED AND 00/100   United States Dollars

for Value received and charge the same to account of

To   DRAWN ON BANK OF CHINA
      JIANGSU BRANCH
      FOR 100 PCT OF INVOICE VALUE   INC.

No.   5314   Authorized Signature

Bank of China
Advice Number 4D06NY1421
LC No. LC9410105260

It is very important to study the documents and compare it to the letter of credit. It is a good idea to have one person who is in charge of the paper transaction to help reduce discrepancies. They cost you time and money and could affect the payment from your customer. If there are any discrepancies you have not corrected, advise your customer right away by e-mail and ask for them to accept them and to advise this back to you in writing. Keep in mind that small discrepancies such as spelling errors are not important but will cost you money if sent. Discrepancies such as the wrong LC number or mistake in the dates used can have a serious effect on your transaction. Always try to meet the expiry dates and ship dates. If you cannot, then you need your customer to amend the letter of credit to allow you more time.

CHAPTER 3

Documentary Collections (D/A,D/P)

Another very simple and safe way you can do an international sale for export is to use D/P (documents against payment). This is a very powerful tool. To use this system, you give instructions to your bank that the documents attached to a sight draft for collection are deliverable to the buyer only against payment. This means the buyer cannot obtain the goods until he pays the bank. Upon payment, he gets to obtain the goods when the bank releases the documents such as bill of lading and invoice.

Using this method is the best way if both parties have a trusting relationship, as it has the advantages of reducing banking cost and paperwork. In addition, it reduces the time required for you to get paid, and it does not tie up money for your customer as do letters of credit. The risk is mainly taken on your side as the seller. If you ship the goods and the customer does not make payment, then you have materials stuck in a foreign country that you will need to have shipped back to you at your expense. So to use the D/P system, you really need to know your customer very well. The good point is you are usually paid before the goods even arrive at the country if the shipment is done by ocean freight. Normally you can receive payment within twenty days. For air freight shipments, payment can be even faster.

A sight draft is payable when presented by your bank to the customer's bank. Money is payable at sight or when the completed documents are presented. All letters of credit and D/P use a sight draft or a bank draft as it shows the exact dollar amount to be paid

Another international collection method is D/A or documents against acceptance. This works the same way that D/P does, but a time draft is used. This means you are giving your customer some extra time to pay, such as thirty days or sixty days after receiving the goods instead of paying right away.

How the D/P system works:

1. Exporter fills out sight draft and documents and sends to your freight forwarder or shipper.
2. Freight forwarder ships goods and obtains bill of lading signed by the actual carrier doing the shipment.
3. Freight forwarder sends documents back to you, and you can forward these documents to your bank.
4. Your bank sends the documents to importer's bank.
5. Importer accepts the documents and approves payment. Importer is given the documents by his bank, and this is proof the goods belong to him so the carrier will release the goods.
6. Importer's bank wire transfers money to exporter's bank. Your bank puts the payment into your account.
7. The transaction is complete.
8. You will be sent a notice of payment.

You will need a good freight forwarder who is certified and knows how to handle your shipments and get bills of lading back to you quickly so you can get paid. If the freight forwarder does not provide fast return service of the bill of lading, then your payment will be delayed, sometimes by as much as one month. To keep your company cash flow in good shape, fast payment is very necessary. So in conclusion, your selection of the bank and the freight forwarder is very important to be successful in international business.

I used this D/P method for years with a Korean Company who would purchase $150,000 worth of material from us every month. We had a distributor agreement with our supplier here in the United States who gave us up to ninety days to pay. Using the documents against payment method, the Korean company paid us within twenty days of the ship date. We would send the documents to the bank right away, and sometimes we were paid in ten days. This gave us a very positive cash flow, allowing us to use the customer's money for up to seventy days.

The following pages show examples of the necessary documents for using D/P or D/A system. The example shows a typical D/A set of documents and how they are worded. Using D/A should only be done if you know the customer well and they have a good history of performance. Of course if your customer is a major international company, such as Samsung or Panasonic, then you have little risk of nonpayment.

Documents that are used for D/P and D/A are:

1. Application of documentary collection
2. Bank cover letter
3. Draft
4. Invoice
5. Packing list
6. Certificate of origin
7. Bill of lading
8. Certificate of analysis
9. Declaration of nonconiferous wood packing material, required for China shipments
10. Copy of customer purchase order or contract
11. Advice letter from your bank that the customer accepted the documents and will make payment

On the following pages in this chapter are examples for D/A transactions:

1. Application of documentary collection, dated September 13, 2005

This shows exactly what documents are being sent to the bank for this transaction and shipment. This document can be obtained from your bank or the bank that will be the advising bank. This document is to be made out by your company as the exporter.

Document examples in chapter 3:

Page 51   Application of documentary collection
Page 52   Bank of China documents for collection letter
Page 54   Draft
Page 56   Invoice 5111
Page 57   Packing list 5111

APPLICATION OF DOCUMENTARY COLLECTION

TO: BANK OF CHINA, NEW YORK BRANCH   DATE: **SEPTEMBER 13, 2005**

We enclose the following specified documents. Please collect in accordance with our instructions indicated herein and the rules stipulated in URC 522. We understand that we will be bound by all the rules stipulated in URC 522 and agree to reimburse you for all your unpaid charges and the charges incurred by your correspondent bank in connection with this collection. We also understand that presentation of document (s) that are not in compliance with the applicable anti-boycott, anti-terrorism, anti-money laundering, and sanctions laws and regulations is not acceptable. Applicable laws vary depending on the transaction and may include United Nations, United States and / or local laws.

COLLECTION INSTRUCTIONS ARE MARKED "X":	COLLECTING BANK (in full address):
☐ deliver documents against payment (D/P) ☒ deliver documents against acceptance (D/A) ☐ do not protest ☐ protest for non-payment/non-acceptance	**BANK OF CHINA – JIANGSU BRANCH** **148 ZHONG SHAN NAN ROAD** **NANJING 210005, JIANGSU PROV.** **CHINA** **ATTN: INT'L DEPT.**

TEL.	DRAWN ON (in full address):
☒ advice non-payment and/or non-acceptance ☒ advice payment ☒ advice acceptance	**HUA FEI COLOUR DISPLAY SYSTEMS CO., LTD.** **P.O. BOX 2808** **MAI GAO QIAO** **NANJING, CHINA 210028**

☐ collect interest from drawee _____ % p.a. from _____ to approximate date proceeds arrived in _____ (basis of 360 days)	TENOR: at **60** days after B/L or AWB date (due date **NOV. 12,2005**)
☐ your correspondent's charges to be paid by drawee	AMT & CURRENCY: **USD12312.48**
☐ collect your charges from drawee ☐ your charges to be paid by us ☒ waive all charges if refused by drawee and charge them to us *DO NOT SHOW BANKING CHARGES ON COVER LETTER*	DISPOSITION OF PROCEEDS: (X) please remit proceeds by chips through **KEY BANK NATIONAL ASSOCIATION** for credit to our A/C no. **350001** quoting Our reference **5111**

OTHER INSTRUCTIONS:	SPECIAL INSTRUCTIONS:
WIRE PROCEEDS TO: **KEY BANK NATIONAL ASSOCATION** **ACCOUNT NAME:** **INC.** **ACCT# 35000** **TELEX: 89=5817 ABA# 041001039**	1. Please request the collecting bank to remit the proceeds by telegraphic transfer. 2. All documents will be sent in one cover by courier designated by you unless otherwise stated.

DOCS	draft	Com Inv.	Cust inv.	Pack list	Qty/ Qlty Cert.	Insp. cert.	Cert. orig.	Ins pol/ cert.	B/L or AWB	NN B/L, AWB	Cert. of anal	Non- Wood Cert.	Cust. P.O.				
NO ENCL	1	3		3			1		2	3	2	1	1				

CONTACT NAME: **MR. RON**   YOURS FAITHFULLY,

APPLICANT: **INC.**
                 1110 PINELLAS
                 SUITE   AUTHORIZED SIGNATURE

TELEPHONE NO.:   **727-**

THIS APPLICATION OF DOCUMENTARY COLLECTION IS SUBJECT TO URC 522

2. Bank of China New York cover letter or the advising bank's cover letter is sent with your documents to the Bank of China Jiangsu Branch in this case or the customer's bank. This is an official bank-to-bank letter that also advises instructions to the customer's bank how to remit payment.

BANK OF CHINA
NEW YORK BRANCH

410 Madison Ave	Tel: (212) 935-3101
New York	Telex: ITT 423635, WU 661723, TRT 177383
NY 10017	S.W.I.F.T.: BKCH US33

```
TO: BANK OF CHINA-JIANGSU BRANCH              DATE: Sep 15 2005
    148 ZHONG SHAN NAN LU
    NANJING 210005, JIANGSU PROV.              OUR REF: BC05NY0796
    CHINA

GENTLEMEN,

         WE ENCLOSE HEREWITH THE FOLLOWING DOCUMENTS FOR COLLECTION.

DRAWN BY                              DRAWN ON
                INC.                  HUA FEI COLOUR DISPLAY SYSTEMS CO.
            BAYWAY SO.                LTD.,
SUITE                                 P.O. BOX 2808, MAO GAO QIAO,
            23715                     NANJING 210028, CHINA
REF. INV. 5111                        P.O. 222912
                                      TENOR: D/A  60 DAYS AFTER B/L DATE
         DOCUMENTS ENCLOSED                 DUE DATE: NOV. 12, 2005
-------------------------------------DRAFT AMOUNT:  USD           12312.48
 2        1 DRAFT
 3        1 COM'L INVOICE
 3        1 PACKING LIST              our chgs USD              150.00
 2        1 CERT OF ANALYSIS
 2        1 CERT OF ORIGIN           TOTAL AMOUNT:  USD          12312.48
 2        1 NON-WOOD CERT                                       12,482.48
 2/3      1 B/L
 3        1 NN B/L                   SPECIAL INSTRUCTIONS:
          1 CABLE/TELEX COPY         1. YOUR CHARGES FOR DRAWEE'S A/C
          1 SHIPPING ADVICE
 1        1 COPY OF CONTRACT

PAYMENT INSTRUCTION:
    -PLEASE AUTHORIZE US TO DEBIT YOUR ACCOUNT WITH US BY SWIFT MT202
    QUOTING OUR REF. BC05NY0796   ON DUE DATE.

ADDITIONAL INSTRUCTIONS:
1. DELIVER DOCUMENTS AGAINST ACCEPTANCE AND ADVISE BY TELEX
   IN CASE OF NON-ACCEPTANCE. PLEASE ACKNOWLEDGE AND ADVISE US THE
   MATURITY DATE ASAP.
2. UNLESS OTHERWISE SPECIFIED THIS COLLECTION IS SUBJECT TO THE UNIFORM
   RULES FOR COLLECTION OF COMMERCIAL PAPER, INTNATIONAL CHAMBER OF
   COMMERCE PUBLICATION NO. 522
3. PLEASE DO NOT COMBINE PAYMENT.

T207
                                     AUTHORIZED SIGNATURES
```

3. The draft clearly shows the payment terms are D/A sixty days after the bill of lading date. This is also stated in the application of documentary collection. You can see the terms mean payment will be made sixty days after the bill of lading date, which is September 12, 2005, and payment is to be made on November 12, 2005.

Bank of China

U.S. $ 12,312.48   SEPTEMBER 13   20 05

D/A 60 DAYS AFTER B/L DATE   of this *FIRST* of Exchange (Second unpaid)

Pay to the Order of   INC.   FL U.S.A.

TWELEVE THOUSAND THREE HUNDRED TWELEVE AND 48/100   **United States Dollars**

for Value received and charge the same to account of

To   HUA FEI COLOUR DISPLAY SYSTEMS CO., LTD.
P.O. BOX 2808 MAI GAO QIAO
NANJING, CHINA

No. 5111   INC.
Authorized Signature

Date

Gentlemen:

We enclose Draft Number _____ and documents below

- ☐ for collection,
- ☐ for
- ☐ for payment/negotiation under L/C

BILLS OF LADING	B/L COPY	COMM. INV.	INS. CTF.	CTF. ORIG.	CONS. INV.	PKNG. LIST	WGT. CTF.	OTHER DOCUMENTS
2	3	3		1		3		Cust. P.O. / Non-wood Cert.

Please handle in accordance with instructions marked "X"

☒ Deliver all documents in one mailing.
☐ Deliver documents in two mailings.
☒ Deliver documents against payment if sight draft, or acceptance if time draft.
☒ All charges for account of drawee.
☐ Do not waive charges.
☒ Protest for ~~non-payment~~ non-acceptance
☐ Do not protest.
☒ Present on arrival of goods.
☒ Advise ~~non-payment~~ non-acceptance by ~~airmail~~ cable giving reasons.
☒ Advise ~~payment~~ acceptance by ~~airmail~~ cable

IN CASE OF NEED refer to:

Name _____

Address _____

who is empowered by us:

a ☐ To act fully on our behalf, i.e., authorize reductions; extensions, free delivery, waiving of protest, etc.

b ☐ To assist in obtaining acceptance or payment of draft, as drawn, but not to alter its terms in any way.

OTHER INSTRUCTIONS:

Please refer all questions concerning this collection to:
☐ Shipper
☐ Freight Forwarder:

_____   _____
                                     Authorized Signature

Form 20-015 Printed and Sold by UNICO 700 Central Ave., New Providence, NJ 07974 • (800) 831-3098

4 and 5. The invoice and packing list are required, and the wording is very important. Usually, the net weight and gross weight must be shown. This is because the bill of lading only shows the gross weight. The gross weight is the total weight of the shipment including as the weight of packing materials such as steel drums or packing wood. These documents must also show the number of pieces and have the correct bill-to and ship-to address.

INC.

1110 SOUTH	
SUITE	
_____ FL 33715 U.S.A.	
PHONE# 1-727-(	

Invoice

Date	Invoice #
8/31/2005	5111

Bill To	Ship To
HUA FEI COLOUR DISPLAY P.O. BOX 2808 MAI GAO QIAO, NANJING CHINA	HUA FEI COLOUR DISPLAY P.O. BOX 2808 MAI GAO QIAO, NANJING CHINA

P.O. No.	Terms	Ship Via
222812	D/A 60 DAYS	OCEAN PREPAID

Description	Unit	Shipped	Price	Amount
UCARCIDE 250 (1322 527 22501) N.W.=20.87KG.EA./ 417.40KG. TOTAL G.W.=21.80KG.EA./ 436.00KG. TOTAL TOTAL PAILS = 20	LTR	454	27.12	12,312.48
Order number should be quoted on all documents and packages. Country of Origin: USA Shipment contains no wood products: The packing material in this shipment contains No wood from coniferous trees. Only wood from deciduous trees has been used, These are in full compliance with China requirements. Shipping mark = HuaFei Payment Terms: D/A 60 days after B/L date CIF Nanjing China Hua Fei Colour Display Systems CO., LTD. Phone: 011-86-25-542-1166 Fax: 011-86-25-541-7470				

ORIGINAL   INC.

Total	$12,312.48
Payable in US DOLLARS	

INC.

SOUTH

SUITE

U.S.A.

PHONE# 1-727-

Packing List

Date	Invoice #
8/31/2005	5111

Bill To
HUA FEI COLOUR DISPLAY
P.O. BOX 2808
MAI GAO QIAO, NANJING
CHINA

Ship To
HUA FEI COLOUR DISPLAY
P.O. BOX 2808
MAI GAO QIAO, NANJING
CHINA

P.O. No.	Terms	Ship Via
222812	D/A 60 DAYS	OCEAN PREPAID

Description	Unit	Shipped
UCARCIDE 250 (1322 527 22501) N.W.=20.87KG.EA./ 417.40KG. TOTAL G.W.=21.80KG.EA./ 436.00KG. TOTAL TOTAL PAILS = 20	LTR	454

Order number should be quoted on all documents and packages.
Country of Origin: USA
Shipment contains no wood products: The packing material in this shipment contains No wood from coniferous trees. Only wood from deciduous trees has been used. These are in full compliance with China requirements.
Shipping mark = HuaFei
Payment Terms: D/A 60 days after B/L date
CIF Nanjing China
Hua Fei Colour Display Systems CO., LTD.
Phone: 011-86-25-542-1166
Fax: 011-86-25-541-7470

ORIGINAL   INC.

6.   Most countries require a certificate of origin.

Certificate of Origin

Inc. hereby certifies and confirms that all products included in this shipment were made in quality and quantity at factories in the United States of America.

Invoice # 5111

HUA FEI - PO # 222812

Commodity	Quantity / Weight
UCARCIDE 250	20 PAILS / 454.00 KG. NET WEIGHT

08/31/05

Original

Inc.

7. The bill of lading shows the gross weight and the type of material and sometimes what the material is used for as this helps expedite customs clearance. In this example, the bill of lading date plus sixty days will be the payment date. A certificate of analysis may also be required.

INTERNATIONAL EXPRESS SHIPPING CO., LTD.

BILL OF LADING

Shipper/Exporter		Document No	B/L NO
INC. SOUTH FL. 33715 U.S.A.		OXIES-6757 Export References 5111	IESNY-943026

Consignee	Forwarding Agent References
HUA FEI COLOUR DISPLY SYSTEMS CO.,LTD. P.O.BOX 2808 MAI GAO QIAO, NANJING, CHINA	
Notify Party	**Port And Country Of Origin** U.S.A.
SAME AS CNEE TEL:011-86-25-542-1166	**Domestic Routing/Export Instructions** DIMERCO ZHONGJING INT'L EXPRESS CO.,LTD. FLAT E, 6TH FL. PHASE 2, EAST OCEAN CENTER 618 YAN AN RAOS EAST, SHANGHAI,CHINA (TEL)862153854886　　(FAX)862153854885

Pre-Carriage By	Place Of Receipt CFS/CHICAGO
Ocean Vessel/Voyage/Flag OOCL/AMERICA　V091	**Port Of Loading** LONGBEACH, CA. U.S.A.
Port Of Discharge SHANGHAI CHINA PORT	**For Transhipment To** NANJING, CHINA

PARTICULARS FURNISHED BY SHIPPER

Container No. / Seal No Marks and Numbers	No. of Cont or Other Pkgs.	Description of Packages and Goods	Gross Weight	Measurement
HUA FEI COLOR DISPLAY SYSTEMS CO.LTD.	1 SKID	"SHIPPER'S LOAD & COUNT" COATING MATERIALS FOR COLOR PICTURE TUBE. UCARCIDE 250 P.O.NO. 222812 COUNTRY OF ORIGIN : U.S.A. FREIGHT PREPAID SHIPMENT CONTAINES NO WOOD PRODUCTS - 20 PAILS PACKED ON 1 HEATED SKID - HAZARDOUS GOODS:CORROSIVE LIQUID, ACIDIC ORGANIC,N.O.S.UN3265 CLASS 8 PG II	1036 LBS 470 KGS	42 CFT 1.177CBM

LADEN ON BOARD:09/12/05
OOCL/AMERICA　V091
LONGBEACH,CA.U.S.A.

THESE COMMODITIES, TECHNOLOGY, OR SOFTWARE WERE EXPORTED FROM THE
UNITED STATES IN ACCORDANCE WITH THE EXPORT ADMINISTRATION
REGULATIONS. DIVERSION CONTRARY TO U.S. LAW PROHIBITED.

ORIGINAL

Freight And Charges			
Revenue Tons Rate Per	Prepaid	Collect	IN ACCEPTING THIS BILL OF LADING, the shipper, owner and consignee of the goods, and the holder of the bill of lading expressly accept and agree to all its stipulations exceptions and conditions, whether written, stamped or printed, as fully as if signed by such shipper, owner, consignee and/or holder. No agent is authorized to waive any of the provisions of the within clauses.
FREIGHT....	AS ARRANGED		IN WITNESS WHEREOF, the master or agent of the said ship has affirmed to THREE bills of lading, all of this tenor and date. ONE of which being accomplished, the others to stand void.

DATED AT　　　　　　　　　　　09/12/05
INTERNATIONAL EXPRESS SHIPPING CO., LTD.

AS AGENT FOR OOCL/DCL AS CARRIER
By　　　　　　　　　　
For and On Behalf of the Master

TOTAL CHARGES

8. If you are shipping chemicals or metals, it will be necessary to have a certificate of analysis.

```
Certificate 2594178        The Dow Chemical Company

Date:  07/29/2005          Certificate of Analysis        Shipped: 8-24-2005


                                                     Dlvy Note: 64455804 40
                                                     Order No. : 08871139

Material:    UCARCIDE(TM) 250 Preservative
             500 LB POLYETHYLENE DRUM                Spec:      00129018-S
Cust Mtl:    0112147

Batch:       TG265554G2
Orig. Batch:

Dlvy Qty:DR  2
Vehicle:     DALE
Ship from:  UNION CARBIDE CORPORATION    INSTITUTE    WV UNITED STATES

This material meets the requirements of the specification.
```

	Units	Results TG265554G2	Limits Minimum	Maximum	Method
Sp. Grav. @ 20/20C	-	1.128	1.123	1.133	ASTM D4052
Glutaraldehyde	% wt	51.0	50.0	51.5	DOWM 102080-E04A
pH at 25degC	-	4.0	3.1	4.5	ASTM E70
Dilution Base Test	% T	0.4	0.0	1.0	1B-4Q5-1
Color, Pt-Co	-	4	0	100	ASTM D1209
Appearance	-	Passes			1B-4Q5-1

```
Quality Coordinator
Biocides

For inquiries please contact Customer Service or local sales
     English: 800-232-2436   French: 800-565-1255

*  Trademark of The Dow Chemical Company
```

9. The declaration of nonconiferous wood packing material letter is required for China shipments. This must also be on the bill of lading. This is to prevent any bugs or termites from coming into China.

Declaration of non-coniferous wood packing material

To the Service of China Entry & Exit Inspection and Quarantine:

It is declared that all wood packing materials in this shipment are made of heat treated non-coniferous trees.

Invoice # 5111

HUA FEI - PO # 222812

Commodity   *Quantity / Weight*

UCARCIDE 250   20 PAILS / 454.00 KG. NET WEIGHT

08/31/05

Original

Inc.

10. The customer contract or purchase order also needs to be included with the documents. This is proof of the price and the payment terms for the items shipped.

FROM :H   FAX NC. :   Aug. 23 2005 15:37   P1

To: Jim Jessie 2005.8.23

HUA FEI CONTRACT   ORIGINAL *

HUA FEI COLOUR DISPLAY SYSTEMS CO., LTD.
HUA FEI ROAD 1, NANJING, P.R.CHINA

ORDER TO: 50002	ORDER REF. NR.:	DEALT WITH BY:
	222812	WANG WEI
INC	GOODS TO BE DELIVERED TO:	TELEPHONE:
		85421166-5165
	HUA FEI COLOUR DISPLAY SYSTEMS CO., LTD.	FAX:
ATTN: MR. J.	P.O.BOX. 2808, MAI QAO QIAO, NANJING.	86-25-85429617
FAX NO: 1-717-	CHINA.	
C/O: 025-5889 1690		P.O.BOX:
	SHIP-TO-FUNLOC: 261323	2808

| TERMS OF DELIVERY: | PRICE TERM: |
| ETA NANJING BEFORE OCT.15TH | CIF |

| TRANSPORT INSTRUCTION: | TERMS OF PAYMENT: |
| BY SEA | D/A 60 AFTER THE MONTH END OF B/L |

PACKING:	DOCUMENTS TO BE SENT:		
PROPERLY PACKED IN SEAWORTHY STANDARD	ORDER CONFIRMATION TO:	WANG WEI	MATERIAL DIVISION
	SIGNED ORDER TO:	WANG WEI	
COUNTRY OF TRADE:	INVOICE COPY TO:	WANG WEI	
P.R.China	INVOICE ORIGINAL TO:	MS. Yang ping	F&A DIVISION

NR.	DESCRIPTION	12NC	PRICE% IN USD	QUANTITY	UNIT	TOTAL PRICE IN USD
1	UCARCIDE 250/21" 25" 29"	1322 527 22501	2,712.000	454.00	LR	12,312.48
					AMOUNT: USD	12,312.48

SELLER'S SIGNATURE & DATE   BUYER'S SIGNATURE & DATE

UPON THE CONTRACT IS SIGNED BY BOTH SELLER AND BUYER, IT WILL BE LEGALLY EFFECTIVE IMMEDIATELY.
ANY PARTY FAILS TO FULFUILL ABOVE CONTRACT TERMS, ANOTHER PARTY HAS RIGHT OF CLAIM ON THE LOSS
RELATED.

2841 207 71002

11. After the documents are submitted, you will receive a letter advising the customer has accepted them. This letter usually comes from your bank within two weeks. Receipt of this letter means your company will be paid within a few days of the date on the letter.

BANK OF CHINA
NEW YORK BRANCH

410 Madison Ave.	Tel: (212) 935-3101
New York	Telex: ITT 423635, WU 661723, TRT 177383
NY 10017	S.W.I.F.T.: BKCH US33

TO: . INC.   DATE: Sep 23 2005

    SUITE 1
           FL   OUR REF: BC05NY0786

  YOUR INV.5111

GENTLEMEN,

    RE: YOUR COLLECTION FOR USD   12312.48
    DRAWN ON HUA FEI COLOUR DISPLAY SYSTEMS CO.

THE SUBJECT ITEM HAS BEEN ACCEPTED BY THE DRAWEE TO DUE ON Nov 14 2005 .

BEST REGARDS.

                           TRULY YOURS

T307

In conclusion, the reader should now have a good knowledge of the way that documentary collection works. Using the examples, one can determine what type of documents are required. The documents required are basically the same as for a letter of credit. The big advantage is you have no letter of credit to read and conform to.

So the use of documents against payment or D/P and documents against acceptance or D/A is a much easier method to use for an international collection. The bank only acts as an in-between, handling the documents and payment between you and your customer. Another nice advantage is that the D/A and D/P method will cost you far less money than a letter of credit payment by your customer. Your customer may like to use D/A or D/P as it means they do not have to have the funds on deposit for a letter of credit. So both customer and supplier benefit from the use of these payment methods.

The only drawback is as the supplier, you really need to know your customer is a reliable trading partner and will pay you on time if using the D/A method. If D/P method, you have less worry as they are required to pay before the release of documents in most countries. This brings up an important point about international trade, and that is to try to find out what are the banking rules in the country you are trading with. This can be found out by contacting your banker.

CHAPTER 4

Net 30 Days and Payment in Advance

Net 30 Days

One can also use Net 30 day terms, just as we do in the United States with a customer. The Net 30 day term is the best method to use if there is a good, trusting relationship. You also need to take into account who the customer is and what the size of their company is. For example, most companies would have no problem giving Panasonic Net 30 or even Net 60 day payment terms. They are a huge international company that can be trusted to pay their invoices on time. Most companies overseas prefer sixty-day payment terms.

The steps to use Net 30 day terms for customers overseas are very easy. It is very similar to doing business in the United States, but you receive payment by wire transfer directly to your bank from the customer's bank overseas instead of a check.

1. The customer sends you an inquiry to purchase a certain material.
2. You send them back a formal quote which contains the payment terms, shipping terms, conditions, item description, specification, and any other information such as an MSDS (material safety data sheet).
3. The customer sends you a purchase order that shows all your terms and conditions and material description.
4. Upon receiving the purchase order, you send a confirmation to the customer that it was received and provide them with an estimated ship date.
5. When goods are ready to ship, notify your shipper to pick up the goods and provide you with an original bill of lading once the goods are on board.
6. E-mail your customer a copy of all the documents, and be sure to put your bank address and SWIFT code with your account number on the invoice.

This is to assure you receive payment. The following example should be on your invoice:

REMIT PAYMENT TO:

KeyBank

127 Public Sq.

Cleveland, Ohio 44144 USA

ABA Routing No. 041 001 039

SWIFT: KEYBUS33

Account No.: 35000

Account Name: Kemco

This address tells the overseas bank exactly how and where to submit payment. It takes about two to three days to receive the funds in your account from the date the customer's bank remits payment.

7. Send your customer the original documents by UPS or express mail. These documents allow the customer to obtain his goods from the shipping company and the customs broker in his country. They show he has Net 30 days to make payment.

8. Now you just wait for payment from your customer and hope he pays on time. There is nothing that can make the customer pay on time, so usually they pay late by up to fifteen days. You really need to trust your customer.

This is a direct sale to your customer, and the bank's only job in this transaction is to transfer funds to your account. If the customer does not pay you, your bank can be of no help in the collection. You will have to either phone or visit the customer to obtain payment if necessary. This is why it is important to know if your customer is a large stable company.

The following pages are examples of the necessary documents to send your customer. In this case, the customer was in Brazil. Each country or customer may require slightly different documents. It is necessary to obtain a list of the documents they will need to clear customs in their country.

On the following pages in this chapter are examples of the following documents, which are submitted for Net 30 Day payment.

1. Customer purchase order
2. Air waybill or bill of lading
3. Commercial invoice
4. Packing list

It may also be necessary to send certifications on any metal or chemicals that are shipped. A bank draft or draft is not necessary with Net 30 day transactions. To check if payment is received, it is necessary to phone your bank, and they will also send you a copy of the wire transfer payment. See the wire transfer advice letter in the following pages.

Document examples in chapter 4:

1. Customer purchase order Net 30 days

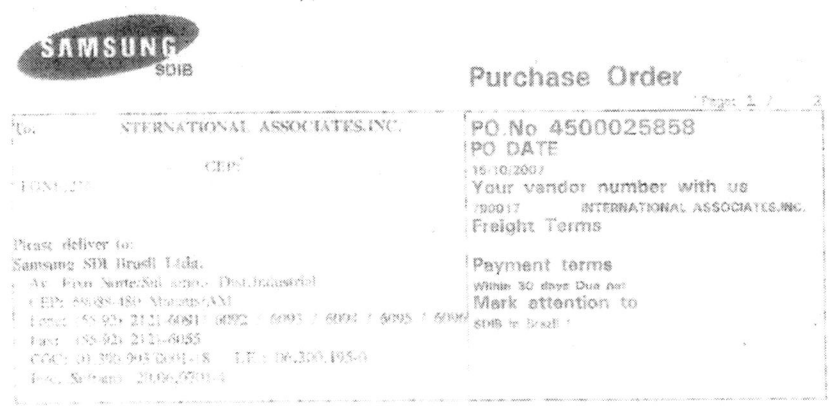

2. Air waybill of lading

Shipper's Name and Address		Shipper's Account Number		Not Negotiable Air Waybill ABSA CARGO	
INC. SOUTH. FL 33715 TEL.: 727-867-				Issued by	
				Copies 1,2, and 3 of the Air Waybill are originals and have the same validity.	
Consignee's Name and Address SAMSUNG SDI BRASIL LTDA AV.EXIO NORTE SUL, S/N DISTRITO INDUSTRIAL, CEP,89086-480,MANAUS-AM,BRASIL				It is agreed that the goods described herein are accepted in apparent good order and condition (except as noted) for carriage SUBJECT TO THE CONDITIONS OF CONTRACT ON THE REVERSE HEREOF. ALL GOODS MAY BE CARRIED BY ANY OTHER MEANS INCLUDING ROAD OR ANY OTHER CARRIER UNLESS SPECIFIC CONTRARY INSTRUCTIONS ARE GIVEN HEREON BY THE SHIPPER, AND SHIPPER AGREES THAT THE SHIPMENT MAY BE CARRIED VIA INTERMEDIATE STOPPING PLACES WHICH THE CARRIER DEEMS APPROPRIATE. THE SHIPPER'S ATTENTION IS DRAWN TO THE NOTICE CONCERNING CARRIER'S LIMITATION OF LIABILITY. Shipper may increase such limitation of liability by declaring a higher value for carriage and paying a supplemental charge if required.	
Issuing Carrier's Agent Name and City NEWTRANS WORLDWIDE, INC. 750 ARTHUR AVE. ELK GROVE VILLAGE, IL 60007 U.S.A.		Accounting Information			
Agent's IATA Code 0118579	Account No.				
Airport of Departure (Addr. of First Carrier) and Requested Routing CHICAGO O'HARE		Reference Number AE-41921		Original Shipper Information	
To	By First Carrier MAO	M3-725 ABSA CARGO	To	by	To	by	Currency USD	CHGS Code P	WT/VAL PPD X COLL	Other PPD X COLL	Declared Value for Carriage N.V.D.	Declared Value for Customs AS ATTACHED
Airport of Destination MANAUS		Requested Flight/Date M3-725 10/25/2007			Amount of Insurance NIL	INSURANCE - If carrier offers insurance, and such insurance is requested in accordance with the conditions thereof, indicate amount to be insured in figures in box marked "amount of insurance".	
Handling Information UPON ARRIVAL PLS. CONTACT MR. ISMAEL COSTA PINHEIRO TEL.: 55-92-2121-6091 FAX.: 55-92-2121-6077							
These commodities, technology or software were exported from the United States in accordance with the Export Administration Regulations. Ultimate destination				Diversion contrary to U.S. law prohibited.			SCI

No. of Pieces RCP	Gross Weight	kg/lb	Rate Class Commodity Item No.	Chargeable Weight	Rate/Charge	Total	Nature and Quantity of Goods (incl. Dimensions or Volume)
1 PIECES	326.1 K			326.1 K	5.45	1,777.25	LK02-20017A TWEEN 20 5 PAILS OROTAN731DP 1 DRUM PLURONIC LR2 5 PAILS
	DIM.: 48 X 48 X 44 X						DETAILS ARE AS PER ATTACHED SHIPPER'S INVOICE NO. 5563
	AES XTN#: 3640840		549-12098866				PO#:4500025858
1 PIECES	326.1 K					1,777.25	"FREIGHT PREPAID"

Prepaid	Weight Charge	Collect	Other Charges				
1,777.25							
	Valuation Charge						
	Tax						
	Total Other Charges Due Agent			#5563 ETA 10/26 MANAUS.			
	Total Other Charges Due Carrier						
277.19			Shipper certifies that the particulars on the face hereof are correct and that insofar as any part of the consignment contains dangerous goods, such part is properly described by name and is in proper condition for carriage by air according to the applicable Dangerous Goods Regulations.				
Total Prepaid		Total Collect	NEWTRANS WORLDWIDE, INC. AS AGENT OF THE				
2,054.44			Signature of Shipper or its Agent				
Executed on (Date)		at (Place)	NEWTRANS WORLDWIDE, INC. AS AGENT OF THE ABSA CARGO 22-Oct-2007 CHICAGO O'HARE		Signature of Issuing Carrier or its Agent		

549-12098866

TOTAL P.01

3. Net 30 day invoice

COMMERCIAL INVOICE

1)Shipper/Exporter		8)No. & date of Invoice		
		5563		October 18, 2007
		9) No. & date of L/C		
33715 U.S.A				
2)For Account & Risk of Messrs		10)L/C issuing bank		
SAMSUNG SDI BRASIL LTDA.		Payment Terms : Within 30 days Due net		
AV. EIXO NORTE SUL, S/N DISTRITO INDUSTRIAL,				
CEP.69088-480, MANAUS-AM, BRASIL				
Attn. Mr.Ismael Costa Pinheiro Phone: (55-92) 2121 6891 Fax: (55 92) 2121 6877				
3)Notify party		11)Remarks		
SAMSUNG SDI BRASIL LTDA.				
AV. EIXO NORTE SUL, S/N DISTRITO INDUSTRIAL,		* MERCADORIA DESTINADA A ZONA FRANCA DE MANAUS		
CEP.69088-480, MANAUS-AM, BRASIL		* Vendor No. 790917		
Attn. Mr.Ismael Costa Pinheiro Phone: (55-92) 2121 6891 Fax: (55 92) 2121 68		Bankers: Keybank National Association		
4)Port of loading	5)Final destination	Account# 36000		
CHICAGO O'HARE	MANAUS-BRASIL	SWIFT: KeyBus33 ABA# 040100		
6)Carrier	7)Departing on or about	* PO : 4600025958		
	Oct.18,2007	* FREIGHT PREPAID		
12)Marks&numbers	13)Description of goods	14)Quantity	15)Unit price	16)Amount
LK02-20017A SURFACTANT;TWEEN 20,- ,19.96KG/44LBS. * PO :4600025958 MADE IN U.S.A Maker: UNIQEMA Address: Wilmington, Delaware	LK02-20017A SURFACTANT;TWEEN 20,- ,19.96KG/44LBS. [Sulfactante;Tween20]	99.80 KGS (PAILS = 5)	USD 14.270	USD 1,424.15
LK02-20019A SURFACTANT;PLURONIC L92,- ,18.14KG/40LBS * PO :4600025958 MADE IN U.S.A. Maker: BASF. Address: MOUNT OLIVE, NJ	LK02-20019A SURFACTANT;PLURONIC L92,- ,18.14KG/40LBS [Sulfactante;pluronic L92]	90.70 KGS (PAILS = 5)	USD 28.250	USD 2,562.28
LK02-20017A SURFACTANT;OROTAN731DP, 91.00KG/200.62LBS. * PO :4600025958 MADE IN U.S.A. Maker: RHOM & HAAS CO. Address: PHILADELPHIA,PA	LK02-20017A SURFACTANT;OROTAN731DP,.. 91.00KG/200.62LBS. [Sulfactante Orotan 731DP]	91.00 KGS (DRUMS = 1)	USD 13.800	USD 1,255.80
N/W: 281.50 Kgs G/W: 301.38 Kgs 1 DRUM & 10 PAILS ON 1 WOODEN SKID TOTAL GROSS WEIGHT = 322.98 Kgs	CPT MANAUS BRAZIL TOTAL			USD 5,252.23
	17)Signed by			

4.   Packing list

PACKING LIST

1)Shipper/Exporter		8)No. & date of invoice		
INC. AAYWAY 33715 U.S.A		5563		October 18, 2007
		9) No. & date of L/C		
				°
SAMSUNG SDI BRASIL LTDA. AV. EIXO NORTE SUL, S/N DISTRITO INDUSTRIAL, CEP.69088-490, MANAUS-AM, BRASIL. Attn.Mr.Ismael Costa Pinheiro Phone: (55-92) 2121 6091 Fax: (86 92) 2121 6095		10) Remarks		
3)Notify party SAMSUNG SDI BRASIL LTDA. AV. EIXO NORTE SUL, S/N DISTRITO INDUSTRIAL, CEP.69088-490, MANAUS-AM, BRASIL. Attn.Mr.Ismael Costa Pinheiro Phone: (55-92) 2121 6091 Fax: (55 92) 2121 6055				
4)Port of loading CHICAGO O'HARE	5)Final destination MANAUS-BRASIL	* PO 4600025858		
6)Carrier	7)Departing on or about October 18, 2007			
12)Marks&numbers	13)Description of goods	14) Quantity	15) Net Weight	16) Gross Weight
LK02-20017A SURFACTANT;TWEEN 20,- .19.96KG/44LBS. * PO :4500025858 MADE IN U.S.A. Maker: UNIQEMA Address: Wilmington, Delaware	LK02-20017A SURFACTANT;TWEEN 20,- .19.96KG/44LBS. [Sulfactante;Tween20]	(PAILS = 5)	99.80Kg	106.25Kg
LK02-20019A SURFACTANT;PLURONIC L92,- .18.14KG/40LBS * PO :4500025858 MADE IN U.S.A. Maker: BASF. Address: MOUNT OLIVE, NJ	LK02-20019A SURFACTANT;PLURONIC L92,- .18.14KG/40LBS [Sulfactante;pluronic L92]	(PAILS = 5)	90.70Kg	97.53Kg
LK02-20017A SURFACTANT;OROTAN731DP, 91.00KG./200.62LBS. * PO :4500025858 MADE IN U.S.A. Maker: RHOM & HAAS CO. Address: PHILADELPHIA,PA	LK02-20017A SURFACTANT;OROTAN731DP, 91.00KG./200.62LBS. [Sulfactante Orotan 731DP]	(DRUMS = 1)	91.00Kg	97.80Kg
//				
N/W: 281.50 Kgs G/W: 301.38 Kgs 1 DRUM & 10 PAILS ON 1 WOODEN SKID TOTAL GROSS WEIGHT = 322.96 Kgs		TOTAL	281.50Kg	301.38Kg
		17)Signed by		

Wire transfer advice letter—This is to advise your company that funds were wired to your account.

OH-01-51-0354
910 Tiedeman Rd
Brooklyn, OH 44144

**KeyBank Wire
Transfer Advice**

Statement Date: 11/16/2007

Questions about this statement
Contact the Wire Transfer
Department at 1-800-447-3817

INC

S STE 105
FL   -1506

Wire Transfer Summary	**Account Number: 35000**

Account Title: INC

Credits on this Statement	
1 Credit Transactions	$5,242.23
Debits on this Statement	
0 Debit Transactions	$0.00
Total Activity in this Statement	$5,242.23

Account Activity Detail	**Activity Date: 11/16/2007**

Transaction Number:	11/16/2007 1111
Fed Reference Number:	1116B1QGC06C0004701116080 9FT01
Credit Amount:	$5,242.23
Received from Bank:	
Originating Bank:	BANCO DO BRASIL, S.A.
Originator:	SAMSUNG SDI BRASIL, LTDA
Beneficiary:	INC.
Bank to Bank Information:	
Originating Reference Number:	SWF OF 07/11/14
Originator to Beneficiary Information:	/INV/5563
	KEYBUS33

Payment in Advance of Shipment

The very best method to use for an overseas sale is to require payment in advance of the shipment or prepaid. In this case, the customer pays before the goods are shipped. This system is used for small orders of less than $1,000 or when the customer is a risk in your opinion.

Steps for payment in advance of shipment are:

a.   Customer sends an inquiry.

b.   Your company quotes a price and terms and conditions which are payment in advance. In this case, it is normal practice for you to pay the freight and include the freight charge in the material cost. Since it is your shipper, use a CIF term which covers insurance so if something happens to the shipment, you are protected.

c.   The customer sends you a purchase order, and you return to him a pro forma invoice. A pro forma invoice is used by the customer in many countries as proof to provide their bank that they need to transfer funds outside of the country for payment of goods to be shipped. Be sure to have your banking information on the pro forma.

d.   The customer remits payment to your account.

e.   Once payment is received, you must ship the goods as stated in the pro forma invoice. However, you now make a commercial invoice which is stamped "paid." Advise your customer the shipping information, and e-mail them the new invoice and packing list as well as the bill of lading. You must also send the original copies by UPS or FedEx.

The following is an example of a pro forma invoice. The only difference is it says "pro forma," and the final or original invoice will say "commercial invoice." Since the pro forma is sent to the customer so they can remit payment before the shipment, it is necessary for you to have your bank information on the pro forma so a wire transfer can take place. It normally takes about three days for a wire transfer to come into your account.

INC.

SOUTH

SUITE 105

U.S.A.

PHONE# 1-727-

Date July 15,2008

PRO FORMA Invoice #5666

Bill To and Ship To: Dip Tech Ltd.

Attention Mr. Lior Davidsohn Ph 972-9-7633080

Atir Yeda 17 st',Kfar Saba 44643, Israel

Customer Purchase Order no. : 2130

Product : TEC-PR-01 reflective ink

Quantity: 1 Kg

Price: USD600.00 plus air freight charge of USD300.00 …Total amount USD900.00

Payment terms: Wire transfer in advance of shipment

Delivery : 10 to 15 days from payment date. Shipping freight prepaid. Customer is responsible for any and all tax or duty in Israel. Shipment door to door.

TOTAL AMOUNT DUE FOR THIS PRO FORMA INVOICE IS USD900.00.

Please remit to: Key National Association-International Operations

127 Public Sq. Cleveland, Ohio 44114 USA

ABA ROUTING NUMBER 041 001 039   SWIFT:KEYBUS33

ACCOUNT NO. 35000   ACCOUNT NAME: INC

Signed by: Tom   , Inc.

CHAPTER 5

Bills of Exchange or Drafts

The bill of exchange is commonly called a draft or bill. In the previous chapters, it was noted that it is necessary to have a draft when doing a letter of credit collection or a documentary collection such as documents against payment method (D/P). Drafts are available from your bank or the advising bank. It is necessary for your office to fill in the draft correctly. The draft is a key document that the bank will use to remit the correct amount to our company.

Drafts are like checks in that there is a small risk that payment will be dishonored. This is why a sight draft is the best method as the title of the goods being shipped will not be transferred until payment is made. If the buyer does not pay, then the exporter must return the goods at his expense. This is the only risk.

A sight draft must be used by the exporter if he feels any risk of nonpayment. For ocean bills of lading or ocean shipments, the bank will not turn over the documents for release until payment is made. Air shipments or air waybills of lading, however, do not need to be presented in order for the buyer to claim the goods. So for air shipments, there is some more risk.

The following is an example of a draft (page 79) used for a document against acceptance or D/A. This is sometimes also called a time draft since it is payable sometime in the future. A time draft is extending credit terms to the buyer. You will need to know what documents your customer will require. The bank will also send an official letter (page 78) to the customer's issuing bank advising what documents are being sent. This letter advises what documents are enclosed for the collection, and it spells out the type of collection and any terms or tenor. In this case, it is D/A sixty days after the bill of lading date. The letter also advises the payment due date of November 12, 2005. The letter is advising the payment instructions and any additional instructions. Additional instructions are to advise receipt. It also states that the collection is subject to the Uniform Rules for Collection of Commercial Paper, International Chamber of Commerce Publication No. 522.

Of course there is a fee from your bank for doing this collection. In this case, it was $150.00 on a $12,312.48 draft. It is normal for bank charges to be paid by your company for charges at your advising bank. The customer pays for bank charges on his side at the issuing bank. There will also be a wire transfer fee of about $20 when the payment is made.

Once you have some experience with a customer and how to make drafts and documents, this can all go very smoothly and is much easier than doing a letter of credit. As I stated, my favorite method to use for collections is documents against payment. This uses a sight draft or payable at sight by the issuing bank. One other point is that each country may have different requirements for the documents that are sent. One must be careful that all the necessary documents are sent; otherwise, payment may be delayed.

A clean draft is when no shipping documents are attached to the draft sent to the remitting bank. The documents are sent together with the goods directly to the buyers. Using a clean draft is very risky if one does not know the buyer or customer. This clean draft is usually used to pay for services and not goods.

Names of parties when using drafts are:

Drawer: This is the party who issues the draft or the seller.
Drawee: This is the party who owes the money to the seller. This is the buyer or customer.
Remitting Bank: This is the seller's bank that is remitting the documents to the presenting bank or collecting bank, which is the buyer's bank.

Collecting or Presenting Bank: This is the customer's or buyer's bank.

So in conclusion, if you know the customer well and they do not have any credit problems, it is best to use the D/A or D/P system with a sight draft or time draft.

Document examples in chapter 5:

BANK OF CHINA
NEW YORK BRANCH

410 Madison Ave.	Tel: (212) 935-3101
New York	Telex: ITT 423635, WU 661723, TRT 177383
NY 10017	S.W.I.F.T.: BKCH US33

TO: BANK OF CHINA-JIANGSU BRANCH   DATE: Sep 15 2005
148 ZHONG SHAN NAN LU
NANJING 210005, JIANGSU PROV.   OUR REF: BC05NY0786
CHINA

GENTLEMEN,

     WE ENCLOSE HEREWITH THE FOLLOWING DOCUMENTS FOR COLLECTION.

DRAWN BY   DRAWN ON
           INC.   HUA FEI COLOUR DISPLAY SYSTEMS CO.
        BAYWAY SQ.   LTD.,
SUITE   P.O. BOX 2808, MAO GAO QIAO,
           33715   NANJING 210028, CHINA
REF. INV. 5111   P.C. 222912
                            TENOR: D/A 60 DAYS AFTER B/L DATE
    DOCUMENTS ENCLOSED   DUE DATE: NOV. 12, 2005

2	DRAFT	DRAFT AMOUNT: USD	12312.48
3	COM'L INVOICE		
3	PACKING LIST	*pm chgs USD*	*150.00*
2	CERT OF ANALYSIS		
2	CERT OF ORIGIN	TOTAL AMOUNT: USD	12312.48
2	NON-WOOD CERT		*12,462.48*
2/3	B/L		
3	NN B/L	SPECIAL INSTRUCTIONS:	
	CABLE/TEELX COPY	1. YOUR CHARGES FOR DRAWEE'S A/C	
	SHIPPING ADVICE		
1	COPY OF CONTRACT		

PAYMENT INSTRUCTION:
 -PLEASE AUTHORIZE US TO DEBIT YOUR ACCOUNT WITH US BY SWIFT MT202
  QUOTING OUR REF. BC05NY0786 ON DUE DATE.

ADDITIONAL INSTRUCTIONS:
1. DELIVER DOCUMENTS AGAINST ACCEPTANCE AND ADVISE BY TELEX
  IN CASE OF NON-ACCEPTANCE. PLEASE ACKNOWLEDGE AND ADVISE US THE
  MATURITY DATE ASAP.
2. UNLESS OTHERWISE SPECIFIED THIS COLLECTION IS SUBJECT TO THE UNIFORM
  RULES FOR COLLECTION OF COMMERCIAL PAPER, INTRNATIONAL CHAMBER OF
  COMMERCE PUBLICATION NO. 522
3. PLEASE DO NOT COMBINE PAYMENT.

T207   AUTHORIZED SIGNATURES

U.S. $ 12,312.48   SEPTEMBER 13   20 05

___D/A 60 DAYS AFTER B/L DATE___   of this *FIRST* of Exchange (Second unpaid)

Pay to the Order of   INC.   FL U.S.A.

___TWELEVE THOUSAND THREE HUNDRED TWELEVE AND 48/100___ **United States Dollars**

for Value received and charge the same to account of

To   HUA FEI COLOUR DISPLAY SYSTEMS CO., LTD.
     P.O. BOX 2808 MAI GAO QIAO
     NANJING, CHINA

No. __5111__   INC.
                                                         Authorized Signature

Bank of China

                                                         Date

Gentlemen: ☐ for collection,

We enclose Draft Number _____ and documents below   ☐ for

                                              ☐ for payment/negotiation under L/C

BILLS OF LADING	B/L COPY	COMM. INV.	INS. CTF.	CTF. ORIG.	CONS. INV.	PKNG. LIST	WGT. CTF.	OTHER DOCUMENTS
2	3	3		1		3		Cus. P.C. / Non-wood Cert.

Please handle in accordance with instructions marked "X"

☒ Deliver all documents in one mailing.
☐ Deliver documents in two mailings.
☒ Deliver documents against payment if sight draft, or acceptance if time draft.
☒ All charges for account of drawee.
☐ Do not waive charges.
☒ Protest for non-payment / non-acceptance
☐ Do not protest.
☒ Present on arrival of goods.
☒ Advise non-payment / non-acceptance by airmail / cable giving reasons.
☒ Advise payment / acceptance by airmail / cable

IN CASE OF NEED refer to:

Name _____
Address _____
who is empowered by us:

a ☐ To act fully on our behalf, i.e., authorize reductions; extensions, free delivery, waiving of protest, etc.

b ☐ To assist in obtaining acceptance or payment of draft, as drawn, but not to after its terms in any way.

OTHER INSTRUCTIONS:

Please refer all questions concerning this collection to:
☐ Shipper
☐ Freight Forwarder:

                                              Authorized Signature

Form 20-015 Printed and Sold by UNISCO 700 Central Ave., New Providence, NJ 07974 • (908) 601-3030

CHAPTER 6

Assignment of Proceeds

One very powerful tool you can use if needed is the assignment of proceeds letter. This is a document that transfers all or part of the letter of credit's proceeds to a third party beneficiary. To receive an assignment of proceeds letter, the letter of credit beneficiary needs to submit in writing a request to the advising bank to assign the funds as stated to a third party. Once this is approved, the advising bank will disperse the funds accordingly upon payment of the letter of credit.

The reason you may need this assignment of proceeds letter may be, for example, if you are purchasing a large dollar amount and your supplier will not provide you the necessary credit. You want to purchase and resell the item or items to your customer for a profit. In this case, you can send this assignment of proceeds letter from your bank to your supplier, which may take care of your credit problem. This proceeds letter will promise payment to your supplier from the proceeds of the letter of credit.

When using an assignment of proceeds letter, it is best to use a confirmed letter of credit for the transaction with your customer as this assures payment for the goods. So what are the advantages?

The assignment assures payment protection for your supplier. Your supplier must agree to the use of the assignment letter.

Example:

Your company wants to purchase $100,000 worth of metal and resell it for $125,000 to a customer in China. Your supplier, however, will only give you credit to cover $50,000; and they want you to pay the balance in cash. So this means $50,000 cash out of your company account, which you may not have on hand.

Solution:

Ask your customer to issue a confirmed letter of credit so you know the payment will be made without any doubt.

Advise your supplier that you have a confirmed letter of credit and would like to do an assignment of proceeds letter, which means when you receive payment on the letter of credit, your bank will transfer the full amount of $100,000 to their account. Or you could also offer to pay $50,000 Net 30 days and $50,000 by the assignment of proceeds letter. Using either method, you are not using up your cash flow in the transaction. So the main advantage of using this assignment letter is it can help your company cash flow. So your company makes $25,000 profit and your supplier is paid and everyone is pleased.

It is interesting to note that your customer does not have any knowledge of the assignment of proceeds letter. This proceeds letter is between your company and your supplier. It is necessary to obtain a letter from your supplier stating that they will accept an assignment of proceeds letter and that they realize that your bank will submit the payment amount to your supplier when the LC is paid. Your bank will need a copy of this letter along with the proceeds letter.

The assignment of proceeds letter is much better to use than a transferable letter of credit mentioned in chapter 1. A transferable LC can be very complicated, and it also gives your supplier the name and address of your customer. Most companies do not want the name of their customer and all those contacts given to any supplier. The supplier can become your competitor.

The following page is one example of an application for assignment of proceeds letter from the Bank of China.

中国银行
Bank of China   APPLICATION FOR ASSIGNMENT OF PROCEEDS

TO: ☐ New York Branch   ☐ Los Angeles Branch
         410 Madison Avenue, New York, NY 10017   444 South Flower Street, Los Angeles, CA 90071

Re: Letter of Credit .... (herein called the "Credit")
       Issued by ....
       Your Advice No : ....

Gentlemen:

We hereby authorize you to pay the proceeds of each draft, drawn by us, payable to your order, under the above-mentioned Credit, for and not exceeding the amount of USD ....
in words: USD ....

to the designated assignee below:
Name: ....
Address: ....

Payment instructions (their banker's name, address, ABA no. and A/C no. etc.): ....

This instrument, and your acceptance thereof, is not a transfer of the Credit, and does not give to the designated assignee any interest therein and does not affect either our or your rights to agree to amendments thereto, the cancellation thereof, or any substitution therefore. We warrant to you that we have not, and will not, by negotiation of drafts or otherwise, assign the right to receive the whole or any part of such proceeds or give any other authorization or direction to make any payment thereof to any third party. We also understand that this instrument is not valid for any kind of collateral.

Please advise the designated assignee of your acceptance of this instrument by sending them a letter of assignment and, in consideration thereof, we agree that this instrument is irrevocable.

We transmit to you herewith the original Credit (including all amendments, if any) and request you to note thereon the foregoing authorization and direction, and also enclose our check for $ .... to cover your charges* for this matter.

Signature(s) guaranteed by: Very truly yours,
(Beneficiary's bank name and address)   Beneficiary Name and address:

....

....

....

....
       Authorized Signature(s)   Authorized Signature(s)

                                         ....
                                         Title(s) of Signer(s)

                                         Account no. with Bank of China:
                                         (if applicable)

                                         ....

*Assignment of Proceeds commission is calculated at 1/8 percent (0.125 percent) on the amount assigned. Minimum charge is USD100.00 (commission paid/collected is non-refundable.) Letter of Assignment will be sent to the Assignee via courier unless specified otherwise by the beneficiary. In that case, it will be subjected to extra postage/courier charges.

By using this assignment of proceeds letter several times with your supplier will provide them the trust in the future to give you the necessary credit. This is a very inexpensive method to improve your cash flow due to lack of credit.

Chapter 7

International Shipping Methods and Export Regulations

As was mentioned before, it is very necessary to have a good international freight forwarder who acts as an agent for the exporter in moving cargo to overseas customers. Transporting goods internationally requires proper documents and correct packing. The freight agent needs to be familiar with the import/export laws and rules of the USA and of foreign countries you are shipping to.

My guidelines for a good freight forwarder are:

They need to be able to handle customs export documents.

They should have a warehouse to act as a staging area before loading onto a boat or airplane.

They must be able to correct any packing problems. Certain hazardous goods require special packing.

They must know what materials might require an export license.

They must file the necessary export declaration papers.

They must be able to pick up goods at your location and ship to their warehouse staging area.

When you receive an inquiry from overseas, you must set the shipping terms. Who is going to pay for the shipment freight charges? How is the material going to be shipped, by air or ocean? Before you can quote the customer, you may need to obtain a freight charge estimate from your freight agent if you are to pay the freight. This charge will need to be added to your invoice price either built into the material cost or listed by itself in the invoice.

If the customer pays the freight, he may have his own freight agent to use or he may want to use your freight agent and bill him. In most cases, it is best to control who will be the freight agent. If the agent does not do the documents correctly and in a timely manner, your letter of credit payment or documents against payment could be delayed by a considerable time.

If shipping using a letter of credit, the freight agent needs to have a copy of the letter of credit, invoice, and packing list so he can prepare the wording correctly in the bill of lading. If shipping by documents against payment or acceptance, the freight agent only needs a copy of the invoice and packing list.

The typical steps for making a shipment are as follows:

1. After you obtain the order and the letter of credit, you must make ready your documents and goods to make the shipment.

2. Send a copy of all documents and the letter of credit to your shipping agent. Advise him when and where to pick up the goods for shipment and what date you need the goods shipped by. This may depend on the letter of credit.

3. Your agent will pick up the goods and make a booking on a ship or plane.

4. He will review the goods in his warehouse for correct packing and quantity.

5. He will issue an ocean bill of lading or an air waybill.
   Note: At this point, it is best to have the agent send you the original bill of lading as fast as possible.

6. After you receive the bill of lading, it needs to be reviewed to make sure it is correct, and then send all required documents to your advising bank by UPS or special delivery so they do not become lost in the mail system. Always make several copies just in case the documents become lost.

Ocean bills of lading provide evidence to the title of the goods being shipped. There are two types of ocean bills, which are nonnegotiable and negotiable. In almost all cases, negotiable is used, and this is stamped right on the bill of lading. Air waybills are only issued in nonnegotiable form since the goods shipped by air need to be delivered right away. This way, the customer can take claim of the goods on delivery. So in shipping by air, one needs to be careful that the customer is trustworthy. Even with a letter of credit, if shipped by air, the customer can obtain the goods before payment is made unless it is a confirmed letter of credit that stipulates payment must be made upon presentation of the air waybill.

In most cases, it is not necessary to have an export license when shipping to countries friendly to the United States. Most goods are shipped and stamped No License Required, or NLR, on the invoice. There are, however, some materials such as certain metals and chemicals that do require an export license; so it is a good idea to check on this with your freight agent. He can provide you the ECCN or Export Control Classification Number, and you then check it with the Bureau of Industry and Security.

If an export license is required, then you will need to apply for one. It takes about sixty days to obtain an export license, and there is a lot of paperwork. The following is an example of the export license application and the statement by ultimate consignee and purchaser. It is necessary to have your customer or consignee sign and date the statement by ultimate consignee and purchaser.

The export license will only be good for the time you specify in the application, and it will only be good for a certain quantity that you have advised the customer will purchase over that time. Some export licenses may only be good for one shipment. An export license is only good for one customer at a time.

If you are shipping the same materials to different customers in the same or different countries, you will need an export license for each customer and country.

Document examples in chapter 7:

OMB NO. 0625-0136

| Form BXA 629P | U.S. DEPARTMENT OF COMMERCE |
| REV 5-80 | BUREAU OF EXPORT ADMINISTRATION |

STATEMENT BY ULTIMATE CONSIGNEE AND PURCHASER

GENERAL INSTRUCTIONS — This form must be submitted by the importer (ultimate consignee shown in Item 1) and by the overseas buyer or purchaser, to the U.S. exporter or seller with whom the order for the commodities described in Item 3 is placed. This completed statement will be submitted in support of one or more export license applications to the U.S. Department of Commerce. All items on this form must be completed. Where the information required is unknown or the item does not apply, write in the appropriate words "UNKNOWN" or "NOT APPLICABLE." If more space is needed, attach an additional copy of this form or sheet of paper signed as in Item 8. Submit form within 180 days from latest date in Item 8. Information furnished herewith is subject to the provisions of Section 12(c) of the Export Administration Act of 1979, 50 USC app. 2411(c), and its unauthorized disclosure is prohibited by law.

1. Ultimate consignee name and address

Name

Street and number

City and Country

Reference (if desired)

2. Request (Check one)

a. ☐ We request that this statement be considered a part of the application for export license filed by

U.S. exporter or U.S. person with whom we have placed our order (order party)

for export to us of the commodities described in item 3.

b. ☐ We request that this statement be considered a part of every application for export license filed by

U.S. exporter or U.S. person with whom we have placed or may place our order (order party)

for export to us of the type of commodities described in this statement, during the period ending June 30 of the second year after the signing of this form, or on _____

3. Commodities

We have placed or may place orders with the person or firm named in Item 2 for the commodities indicated below:

COMMODITY DESCRIPTION	(Fill in only if to be checked) QUANTITY	VALUE

4. Disposition or use of commodities by ultimate consignee named in Item 1 (Check and complete the appropriate box(es))

We certify that the commodity(ies) listed in Item 3:

a. ☐ Will be used by us (as capital equipment) in the form in which received in a manufacturing process in the country named in Item 1 and will not be reexported or incorporated into an end product.

b. ☐ Will be processed or incorporated by us into the following product(s) _____ (Specify)

to be manufactured in the country named in Item 1 for distribution in _____ (Name of country or countries)

c. ☐ Will be resold by us in the form in which received in the country named in Item 1 for use or consumption therein. The specific end use by my customer will be _____ (Specify, if known)

d. ☐ Will be reexported by us in the form in which received to _____ (Name of country(ies))

e. ☐ Other (Describe fully) _____

NOTE: If Item 2b is checked, acceptance of this form by the Office of Export Licensing as a supporting document for a future application will be conditioned on its acceptability to support the commodities to which the item applies unless specific approval has been obtained from the Office of Export Licensing for such request.

(Reproduction of this form is permissible, providing that content, format, size and color of paper are the same)

Please continue form and sign certification on reverse side.

USDOC/BXA 08-2430

5. Nature of business of ultimate consignee named in Item 1 and his relationship with U.S. exporter named in Item 2.

 a. The nature of my usual business is — _____ (Broker, distributor, fabricator, manufacturer, wholesaler, retailer, etc.)

 b. Our business relationship with the U.S. exporter is _____ (Contractual, franchise, exclusive distributor, distributor, wholesaler, continuing and regular individual transaction business, etc.)

 and we have had this business relationship for _____ years.

6. Additional information (Any other material facts which will be or value in considering application for license named by this statement.)

7. Assistance in preparing statement (Names of persons other than employees of consignee or purchaser who assisted in the preparation of this statement.)

8. CERTIFICATION OF ULTIMATE CONSIGNEE AND PURCHASER: This item is to be signed by the ultimate consignee shown in Item 1 and by the purchaser where the latter is not the same as the ultimate consignee. Where the ultimate consignee is unknown, this item should be signed by the purchaser.)

We certify that all of the facts contained in this statement are true and correct to the best of our knowledge and belief and we do not know of any additional facts which are inconsistent with the above statement. We shall promptly send a supplemental statement to the person named in Item 2, disclosing any change of facts or intentions set forth in this statement which occurs after the statement has been prepared and forwarded. Except as specifically authorized by the U.S. Export Administration Regulations, or by prior written approval of the U.S. Department of Commerce, we will not reexport, resell, or otherwise dispose of any commodities listed in Item 4 above; (1) to any country not approved for export as brought to our attention by means of a bill of lading, commercial invoice, or any other means; or (2) to any person if there is reason to believe that it will result directly or indirectly, in disposition of the commodities contrary to the representations made in this statement or contrary to U.S. Export Administration Regulations.

Ultimate Consignee	Purchaser
Signature in Ink _____ (Signature of official of ultimate consignee)	Signature in Ink _____ (Signature of official of purchaser firm)
Type or print _____ (Name and title of official of ultimate consignee)	Type or print _____ (Name and title of official of purchaser firm)
Date _____	Type or print _____ (Name of purchaser firm)
	Date _____

9. CERTIFICATION FOR USE OF U.S. EXPORTER in certifying that any corrections, additions, or alterations on this form was made prior to the signing by the ultimate consignee and purchaser in Item 8.

We certify that no corrections, additions, or alterations were made on this form by us after the form was signed by the ultimate consignee/ (purchaser).

| Type or print _____ (Name of exporter firm) | Sign here in Ink _____ (Signature of person authorized to certify for exporter. |
| Date signed _____ | Type or print _____ (Name and title of person signing this document) |

The making of any false statement, the concealment of any material fact, or failure to file required information may result in denial of participation in U.S. export. Note: no governmental verification is not assumed.

The following is an actual copy of an export license issued in 1990. It is necessary for you to provide your freight agent a copy of this. The bill of lading needs to have the same description and consignee name, and the export license number needs to be put on all documents. This information also needs to be put into the SED or Shipper's Export Declaration, which is discussed next.

EXPORT LICENSE D105975
VALIDATED: JUL 17 1990
EXPIRES: JUL 31 1992

UNITED STATES DEPARTMENT OF COMMERCE
BUREAU OF EXPORT ADMINISTRATION
P.O. Box 273, Ben Franklin Station
Washington, DC 20044

THIS LICENSE AUTHORIZES THE LICENSEE TO CARRY OUT THE EXPORT TRANSACTION
DESCRIBED ON THE LICENSE (INCLUDING ALL ATTACHMENTS). IT MAY NOT BE
TRANSFERRED WITHOUT PRIOR WRITTEN APPROVAL OF THE OFFICE OF EXPORT
LICENSING. THIS LICENSE HAS BEEN GRANTED IN RELIANCE ON REPRESENTATIONS
MADE BY THE LICENSEE AND OTHERS IN CONNECTION WITH THE APPLICATION FOR EXPORT
AND IS EXPRESSLY SUBJECT TO ANY CONDITIONS STATED ON THE LICENSE, AS WELL AS
ALL APPLICABLE EXPORT CONTROL LAWS, REGULATIONS, RULES, AND ORDERS. THIS
LICENSE IS SUBJECT TO REVISION, SUSPENSION, OR REVOCATION WITHOUT PRIOR NOTICE.

APPLICANT CONTROL NUMBER: C441495

KIA INC   PURCHASER:
25935 DETROIT RD
SUITE #333
WESTLAKE, OH 44145

ULTIMATE CONSIGNEE: INTERMEDIATE CONSIGNEE:
KUMHO ELECTRIC CO LTD
418 MAPO-DONG
MAPO-KU
SEOUL, SOUTH KOREA

COMMODITIES: TOTAL
     QTY DESCRIPTION   ECCN   PRICE

     60000 (QUANTITY = 4801 LBS) ZIRCONIUM STRIP SIZE: 3604 $138,000
       0.127 MM X 4MM

                                            TOTAL: $138,000

PROCESSING CODE: CM

THE EXPORT ADMINISTRATION REGULATIONS REQUIRE YOU TO TAKE THE FOLLOWING ACTIONS
WHEN EXPORTING UNDER THE AUTHORITY OF THIS LICENSE.

     A. RECORD THE EXPORT COMMODITY CONTROL NUMBER IN THE BLOCK
        PROVIDED ON EACH SHIPPER'S EXPORT DECLARATION (SED).

     B. RECORD YOUR VALIDATED LICENSE NUMBER IN THE BLOCK
        PROVIDED ON EACH SED.

     C. PLACE A DESTINATION CONTROL STATEMENT ON ALL BILLS OF LADING,
        AIRWAY BILLS, AND COMMERCIAL INVOICES.

RIDERS AND CONDITIONS:

     1. APPLICANT MUST INFORM CONSIGNEE AND END-USER OF ALL LICENSE

EXPORT LICENSE D105975
    VALIDATED: JUL 17 1990
    EXPIRES: JUL 31 1992

UNITED STATES DEPARTMENT OF COMMERCE
BUREAU OF EXPORT ADMINISTRATION
P.O. Box 273, Ben Franklin Station
Washington, DC 20044

CONDITIONS.

2. THE COMMODITIES AUTHORIZED FOR EXPORT BY THIS LICENSE/AUTHORIZATION
    ARE NOT TO BE USED BY NUCLEAR END USERS OR FOR NUCLEAR END USES.

3. NO RESALE, TRANSFER, OR REEXPORT OF THE COMMODITIES OR DATA LISTED ON
    THIS LICENSE IS AUTHORIZED WITHOUT PRIOR AUTHORIZATION BY THE U.S.
    GOVERNMENT.

Note the riders and conditions spelled out in the export license.

The Shipper's Export Declaration or SED is needed for all shipments over $2,500 and any shipment that requires an export license. The SED is normally filled out by your freight agent and must be presented to the carrier before the shipment can be made. It is now filed electronically at *www.aesdirect.gov*. The SED is now called the EEI or Electronic Export Information. See the following letter on AES (Automated Export System) export processing. Once again, your freight agent should be able to handle this requirement.

29 July 2008

AES Export Processing
for U.S. Department of Commerce and Census Bureaus

To Our Valued Customers,

The U.S. Department of Commerce & CENSUS Bureau has published a new regulation making it mandatory for all U.S. Exporters to file their Electronic Export Information (EEI), formerly referenced as Shippers Export Declaration (SED), using an automated system known as the Automated Export System (AES).

The new rule went into effect on July 2nd with full implementation of the rule set for September 30, 2008. All shippers and carriers exporting from the U.S. must be compliant with all AES policies and procedures. Non-compliance will result in fines and penalty fees from the U.S. government. The countdown to the September 30th enforced compliance deadline is currently at 63 days.

Here's how it works:

The U.S. Principal Party in Interest (USPPI) or designated agent submits EEI via AES to the U.S. Census and receives an ITN (Internal Transaction Number). If the USPPI has Post Departure Filing Privileges (previously referred to as Option 4) or if the cargo is exempt or excluded from AES filing, advance filing is not required; however, the USPPI or designated agent must provide one of the following to the exporting carrier:

- AES Proof of Filing Citation - Internal Transaction Number (ITN)
- AES Post Departure Citation – the Export Transaction Number (XTN) is no longer acceptable
- Exemption or Exclusion Legend

The USPPI will need to submit this required certification on a shipping instruction to Maersk prior to the cargo cutoff. The AES Rule requires that all exporting carriers receive one of the above listed before a loaded container is allowed to be loaded to a vessel for export from a U.S. port.

Please note: Exporting carrier cannot accept paper Shippers Export Declarations

Over the coming weeks as we align our own internal procedures with the AES policy, you will receive additional communication including details on how and when Maersk will specifically require receipt of necessary information from our customers. Until then, for additional information please navigate to the following locations for detailed information on AES:

- AES Official Notice: http://www.census.gov/foreign-trade/aes/mandatory/mandatoryaes-english-20080530.pdf

- AES FAQs: http://www.census.gov/foreign-trade/regulations/faqs/index.html

- AESdirect.gov: http://www.aesdirect.gov/

- Federal Register: Foreign Trade Regulations: Mandatory Automated Export System Filing for All Shipments Requiring Shipper's Export Declaration Information; Final Rule: http://www.census.gov/foreign-trade/regulations/regs/regulations20080602-federalregister.pdf

- For more information about these requirements, please visit: http://www.census.gov/foreign-trade/www/

Some other important points for export shipping are:

1. The export packing list must contain the net weight of the goods and the gross weight of the shipment. The gross weight includes packing materials and any pallets used.

2. Goods should be marked with the invoice number, LC number, and bill of lading number.

3. The goods, as well as the invoice should be marked with the country of origin.

4. For your protection, it is advisable to carry insurance on the goods to cover the cost of any damage during shipment. Normally marine insurance is equal to 110 percent of the invoice value. This is offered by your freight agent who obtains it from a maritime insurance company. Insurance is cheap and provides you protection in case the ship sinks or becomes involved in some type of accident that may damage or lose your goods.

5. Sometimes it is necessary to repackage your goods depending upon what your freight agent advises.

The final remaining problem is how you will ship the goods and who pays for the freight. This must be decided in negotiations with your customer before he places the order. The following is the common glossary for terms of sale, taken from *www. marad.dot.gov.*

Terms of Sale

The point at which sellers have fulfilled their obligations so the goods in a legal sense could be said to have been delivered to the buyer. They are shorthand expressions that set out the rights and obligations of each party when it comes to transporting the goods. Following, are the thirteen terms of sale in international trade as Terms of Sale reflected in the recent amendment to the International chamber of Commerce Terms of Trade (INCOTERMS), effective July 1990: exw, fca, fas, fob, cfr, cif, cpt, cip, daf, des, deq, ddu and ddp.

—   EXW (Ex Works) (. . . Named Place): A Term of Sale which means that the seller fulfills the obligation to deliver when he or she has made the goods available at his/her premises (i.e., works, factory, warehouse, etc.) to the buyer. In particular, the seller is not responsible for loading the goods in the vehicle provided by the buyer or for clearing the goods for export, unless otherwise agreed. The buyer bears all costs and risks involved in taking the goods from the seller's premises to the desired destination. This term thus represents the minimum obligation for the seller.

— FCA (Free Carrier) (. . . Named Place): A Term of Sale which means the seller fulfills their obligation when he or she has handed over the goods, cleared for export, into the charge of the carrier named by the buyer at the named place or point. If no precise point is indicated by the buyer, the seller may choose, within the place or range stipulated, where the carrier should take the goods into their charge.

— FAS (Free Alongside Ship) (. . . Named Port of Shipment): A Term of Sale which means the seller fulfills his obligation to deliver when the goods have been placed alongside the vessel on the quay or in lighters at the named port of shipment. This means that the buyer has to bear all costs and risks of loss of or damage to the goods from that moment.

— FOB (Free On Board) (. . . Named Port of Shipment): An International Term of Sale that means the seller fulfills his or her obligation to deliver when the goods have passed over the ship's rail at the named port of shipment. This means that the buyer has to bear all costs and risks to loss of or damage to the goods from that point. The FOB term requires the seller to clear the goods for export.

— CFR (Cost and Freight) (. . . Named Port of Destination): A Term of Sale where the seller pays the costs and freight necessary to bring the goods to the named port of destination, Terms of Sale but the risk of loss of or damage to the goods, as (continued) well as any additional costs due to events occurring after the time the goods have been delivered on board the vessel, is transferred from the seller to the buyer when the goods pass the ship's rail in the port of shipment. The CFR term requires the seller to clear the goods for export.

— CIF (Cost, Insurance and Freight) (. . . Named Place of Destination): A Term of Sale where the seller has the same obligations as under the CFR but also has to procure marine insurance against the buyer's risk of loss or damage to the goods during the carriage. The seller contracts for insurance and pays the insurance premium. The CIF term requires the seller to clear the goods for export.

— CPT (Carriage Paid To) (. . . Named Place of Destination): A Term of Sale which means the seller pays the freight for the carriage of the goods to the named destination. The risk of loss of or damage to the goods, as well as any additional costs due to events occurring after the time the goods have been delivered to the carrier, is transferred from the seller to the buyer when the goods have been delivered into the custody of the carrier. If subsequent carriers are used for the carriage to the agreed upon destination, the risk passes when the goods have been delivered to the first carrier. The CPT term requires the seller to clear the goods for export.

— CIP (Carriage and Insurance Paid To) (. . . Named Place of Destination): A Term of Sale which means the seller has the same obligations as under CPT, but with the addition that the seller has to procure cargo insurance against the buyer's risk of loss of or damage to the goods during the carriage. The seller contracts for insurance and pays the insurance premium. The buyer should note that under the CIP term the seller is required to obtain insurance only on minimum coverage. The CIP term requires the seller to clear the goods for export.

— DAF (Delivered At Frontier) (. . . Named Place): A Term of Sale which means the sellers fulfill their obligation to deliver when the goods have been made available, cleared for export, at the named point and placed at the frontier, but before the customs Terms of Sale border of the adjoining country. (continued)

— DDU (Delivered Duty Unpaid) (. . . Named Port of Destination): A Term of Sale where the seller fulfills his obligation to deliver when the goods have been made available at the named place in the country of importation. The seller has to bear the costs and risks involved in bringing the goods thereto (excluding duties, taxes and other official charges payable upon importation) as well as the costs and risks of carrying out customs formalities. The buyer has to pay any additional costs and to bear any risks caused by failure to clear the goods for in time.

— DDP (Delivered Duty paid) (. . . Named Port of Destination): "Delivered Duty Paid" means that the seller fulfills his obligation to deliver when the goods have been made available at the named place in the country of importation. The seller has to bear the risks and costs, including duties, taxes and other charges of delivering the goods thereto, clear for importation. While the EXW term represents the minimum obligation for the seller, DDP represents the maximum.

— DES (Delivered Ex Ship) (. . . Named Port of Destination): A Term of Sale where the seller fulfills his/her obligation to deliver when the goods have been made available to the buyer on board the ship, uncleared for import at the named port of destination. The seller has to bear all the costs and risks involved in bringing the goods to the named port destination.

— DEQ (Delivered Ex Quay, [Duty Paid]) (. . . Named Port of Destination): A Term of Sale which means the DDU term has been fulfilled when the goods have been available to the buyer on the quay (wharf) at the named port of destination, cleared for importation. The seller has to bear all risks and costs including duties, taxes and other charges of delivering the goods thereto.

In over twenty years of doing business overseas, we have only used CFR, CIF, FOB, and EXW. It is suggested that if you are paying the freight to use CIF and pay a little extra for the insurance protection, just in case some accident happens during shipment. If the customer pays the freight, then FOB or EXW can be used, but make sure they understand the rules, that they are responsible for the goods once loaded, and if any damage happens during shipment or the goods become lost, the problem is theirs. This means they still have to pay you if anything happens. It is a good idea to send them a copy of the definitions. As you can see, shipping is very involved; and if you have a good freight agent, he can save you a lot of work, time, and money.

CHAPTER 8

Summary and Review

In review, we can see that selling and shipping overseas is not as easy as selling in the United States. Reading this book has now made you an expert in international transactions. Not too many people know how letters of credit or documentary collections work. Even fewer know how important a good freight agent can be to help your international selling effort.

Big companies have import and export departments that handle these international sales efforts. It is necessary for the sales department and accounting department to handle all the paperwork involved. It is recommended that one person be in charge of setting up a system in your office. It should be the sales department that makes any major decisions regarding the method of collection since they are the ones in contact with the overseas customer. Now we will review what the important points are in this book.

Chapter 1 Letters of Credit

The best type of letter of credit to use is an irrevocable confirmed letter of credit. This is the only type of LC that will guarantee payment. A confirmed letter of credit means the buyer's bank adds its commitment to honor the payment terms to the supplier's bank. As long as all the documents are correct and the goods have been shipped within the time requirements, you will be paid. This type of LC is used when you have a new customer or are unsure about his ability to pay as required. To obtain this type of letter of credit, you need to advise your customer that your company requires a confirmed letter of credit in order to do business. After the customer has proven they are honest and have continued business with your company, then you can change to an irrevocable LC.

One other key point is using the correct advising bank to handle your side of the letter of credit. It can be your company bank if they have a relationship with the issuing bank. Or it could also be a USA branch of the issuing bank. For example, Bank of China New York Branch is ideal to handle letters of credit from one of their Chinese branches.

Chapter 2 Letter of Credit Discrepancies

Chapter 2 explained discrepancies and how they can cost you money and other problems. This chapter advised how to correct these errors, typing mistakes, or possibly misspellings. Your advising bank is the key to making corrections. I also advise you to check all the documents two or three times before sending them to the advising bank.

Chapter 3 Documentary Collections

There are several documentary types of collection that can be used. The best and safest method is the D/P or documents against payment method. As explained in chapter 3, this is a very safe method to use when there is any doubt about the customer paying. This method uses a sight draft that means the bank will not release the documents until the customer pays. Another added advantage is that the D/P system is very low cost for you and your customer. In most cases, you can receive payment within thirty days of your ship date, and sometimes payment is even faster.

D/A or documents against acceptance works the same way as the D/P, but a time draft is used. This allows the customer a certain time to pay such as thirty days or sixty days. This is also a safe method to use but requires you to know your customer very well.

Chapter 4 Net 30 Days and Payment in Advance

Net 30 days and payment in advance do not make use of documents as do letters of credit and documentary collections methods. Net 30 days is a direct payment system used by you and your customer. The payment goes through the banks, but in this case, they only act to transfer the funds. Using Net 30 day terms requires full trust in your customer to make the required payment on time.

Payment in advance of shipment is the best possible method to use for safety. You receive the payment and then you make the shipment. The risk is zero. Net 30 day terms are very risky. In both methods, keep in mind that documents do not go through the bank but directly from you to the customer.

Chapter 5 Bills of Exchange or Drafts

In chapter 5, we provided examples of different types of drafts. The sight draft used with letters of credit and documents against payment (D/P) system is a powerful tool that requires the customer to pay for the goods when the documents are presented by his bank. This is the safest method to use. If the customer does not pay, then he does not receive the goods, which can then be shipped back to you at your expense. Where do you obtain bank drafts? You can obtain them from your advising bank just by making a phone call. It is necessary for your company to fill in the draft and send it with the other documents to the advising bank. Without a draft, your documents are not complete and you cannot be paid.

Chapter 6 Assignment of Proceeds

The assignment of proceeds letter is a tool that can help you with your supplier payment. If the purchase from your supplier is over your credit limit, you can suggest to them that you use an assignment of proceeds letter against the letter of credit you have from your customer. Your supplier must agree in writing to accept this assignment. If you ask your bank, they will send you the standard assignment of proceeds letter. You fill it out and return it to the bank, and they will send a copy to your supplier. The letter promises to make payment to your supplier as soon as the LC is paid. Using this tool can help reduce your cash flow problems and keep good relations with your supplier.

Chapter 7 International Shipping Methods and Export Regulations

As I mentioned before, it is very necessary to have a good international freight forwarder who acts as an agent for the exporter in moving cargo to overseas customers. Transporting goods internationally requires proper documents and correct packing.

The freight agent needs to be familiar with the import/export laws and rules of the USA and of foreign countries you are shipping to. In most cases, it is not necessary to have an export license when shipping to countries friendly to the United States. Most goods are shipped and are stamped No License Required, or NLR on the invoice. There are, however, some materials such as certain metals and chemicals that do require an export license; so it is a good idea to check on this with your freight agent. He can provide you the ECCN or Export Commodities Classification Number, and you can then check it with the Bureau of Industry and Security. In over twenty years of doing business overseas, we have only used CFR, CIF, FOB, and EXW. It is suggested that if you are paying the freight to use CIF and pay a little extra for the insurance protection, just in case some accident happens during shipment. If the customer pays the freight, then FOB or EXW can be used, but make sure they understand the rules, that they are responsible for the goods once loaded, and if any damage happens during shipment or the goods become lost, the problem is theirs. This means they still have to pay you if anything happens to the shipment. It is a good idea to send them a copy of the freight terms' definitions. This assures there is a complete understanding between both parties. As you can see, shipping is very involved; and if you have a good freight agent, it can save you a lot of work, time, and money.

Summary

Armed with the information in this book, you can be a better manager and business owner. You can control your international exports in a safe manner and not worry about the risk of nonpayment. Remember, always know your customer and his business. I suggest that you always visit your customer to see firsthand their business operations and to help develop good relations.

REFERENCES

Glossary of Shipping Terms: www.marad.dot.gov/publications/glosary/Glossary.html

International Bank Account Number: http://en.wikipedia.org/wiki/IBAN

National Information Center: www.ffiec.gov

Glossary of Trade and Shipping Terms: www.tradeport.org/library/a.html

Export 911: www.export911.com

Transporting Goods Internationally: www.sba.gov

UCC (Uniform Commercial Code): www.law.cornell.edu

Understanding and Using Letters of Credit, Part 1: www.crfonline.org

Letter of Credit: http://en.wikipedia.org/wiki/Letters_of_credit

AES Export Processing: www.census.gov/foreign-trade/aes/mandatory/mandatoryaes-english-20080530.pdf

AES Direct: www.aesdirect.gov

United States Department of Commerce

INDEX

CPSIA information can be obtained at www.ICGtesting.com
Printed in the USA
LVOW07*1143210215

427745LV00010B/105/P